STAR WARS
INSIDER™

ROGUES, SCOUNDRELS,
AND BOUNTY HUNTERS

TITAN
WWW.TITAN-COMICS.COM

Star Wars Insider
Rogues, Scoundrels, and Bounty Hunters

ISBN: 9781785866425

Published by Titan
A division of
Titan Publishing Group Ltd.,
144 Southwark Street,
London, SE1 0UP

First Edition September 2019
10 9 8 7 6 5 4 3 2 1

Printed in China.

Acknowledgments
Titan would like to thank the cast and crews of the *Star Wars* saga. A huge thanks also to Brett Rector and Michael Siglain at Lucasfilm, and Eugene Paraszczuk, Shiho Tilley, and Christopher Troise at Disney for all of their invaluable help in putting this volume together.

Please note:
The interviews and features collected in this volume were originally printed in *Star Wars Insider*, some of which date back over 20 years. In order to maintain the originalty of the material, we have not modified the content unless absolutely neccesary.

ROGUES, SCOUNDRELS, AND BOUNTY HUNTERS

CONTENTS

BOUNTY HUNTERS

006 BOBA BEGINS
The real life origin of the galaxy's most formidable bounty hunter revealed.

012 CLASSIC: HE'S WORTH A LOT TO ME!
An appreciation of Kenner's classic action figure.

014 BOBA FETT: A BOUNTY HUNTER'S JOURNEY
The history of the bounty hunter via comic, books, and screen appearances.

020 ON THE TRAIL OF THE BOUNTY HUNTERS
The actors behind the bounty hunters of *The Empire Strikes Back* discuss their roles.

028 BOBA FETT: FROM OBSCURE VILLAIN TO CULTURAL ICON
Star Wars creators analyze the appeal of Boba Fett.

034 RETRO: BOBA'S BOUNTY
A selection of collectibles from masks to bobbleheads!

036 THE UNUSUAL SUSPECTS
The bounty hunters of *Star Wars: The Clone Wars*.

042 SET PIECE: KAMINO LANDING PLATFORM
Jango Fett battles Obi-Wan Kenobi in an epic confrontation.

044 IT'S STILL NOT EASY BEING GREEDO
Actor Paul Blake on playing the Rodian bounty hunter.

046 BAR ROOM BLITZ!
Maria De Aragon on her role in bringing Greedo to life.

048 DOWN UNDERWORLD
Actress Leanna Walsman on being Zam Wesell.

056 MY *STAR WARS*: JAIME KING
The voice of Aurra Sing speaks out.

058 PREDATORS OF THE EMPIRE
Essential trivia on the greatest bounty hunters.

068 MY *STAR WARS*: SIMON PEGG
The voice of Dengar discusses his *Star Wars* likes.

070 ROGUE'S GALLERY: WHO'S WHO IN JABBA'S PALACE
Meet some of the galaxy's biggest bad guys.

072 A FALL OF SHADOWS
The true story behind 1996's *Shadows of the Empire*.

ROGUES AND SCOUNDRELS

086 HERO
An interview with Han Solo himself, actor Harrison Ford.

092 ROOWARRAGH!
Peter Mayhew on being Chewbacca.

096 LET THE WOOKIEE WIN!
A special report on Chewie's lifetime achievement award at the MTV awards.

100 RETRO: WHAT A WOOKIEE!
Crucial collectibles from slippers to statues!

102 PETER MAYHEW: FANTASY FUZZBALL
The actor behind the Wookiee looks back.

108 20 REASONS WE LOVE CHEWBACCA
Chewie's greatest moments.

116 GOING SOLO: THE SUOTAMO STORY
The actor behind the fur on stepping into the shoes of Peter Mayhew.

122 HARRISON FORD: WHAT LIES AHEAD
Harrison Ford discusses his illustrious career.

126 REMEMBERING BRIAN DALEY
A tribute to the author of the Han Solo trilogy of spin-off novels.

134 SOLO RETURNS
The making of Marvel's Han Solo comic book.

140 APHRA TAKES FLIGHT
An in-depth look at the making of the heart-stopping speeder bike chase.

146 MY *STAR WARS*: BILLY DEE WILLIAMS
An interview with the galaxy's suavest scoundrel.

148 CAPES MAKETH THE CALRISSIAN
The costumes of *Solo: A Star Wars Story*.

154 LANDO'S PRIDE AND JOY
A look around Lando's *Millennium Falcon*.

158 JONATHAN KASDAN: WRITING *SOLO: A STAR WARS STORY*
Creating an early adventure of Han, Chewie, and the gang.

166 FIGHTING TALK
Creating the action in *Solo: A Star Wars Story*.

170 FRINGE APPEAL
Why we love the outsiders of the *Star Wars* saga.

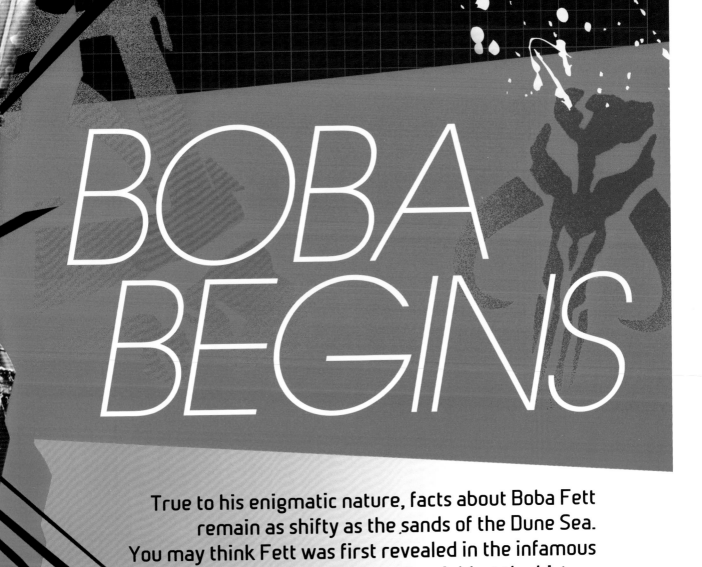

BOBA BEGINS

True to his enigmatic nature, facts about Boba Fett
remain as shifty as the sands of the Dune Sea.
You may think Fett was first revealed in the infamous
1978 *Star Wars Holiday Special,* but the history
of Proto-Fett tells a very different story.

Words: Pete Vilmur

Before *Attack of the Clones*, the origin of notorious bounty hunter Boba Fett had long been a subject of controversy. Was he a vestige of the Clone army, a Mandalorian mercenary, or a super-stormtrooper? Was he once called Jaster Mereel? Did he in fact survive the treacherous Pit of Carkoon? While some of these questions have been answered by the prequels and framers of the Expanded Universe, the character's cinematic debut is still open to debate: is Episode II to be considered the film that launched the Fett character, or was it *The Empire Strikes Back*? And let's not forget about his cameo in the retro-fitted special edition of *Star Wars*.

As for Fett's first public unveiling, tradition holds that Boba was first revealed to audiences as an animated character in 1978's televised *Star Wars* Holiday Special. However, in digging through the records at Skywalker Ranch, a different story emerges. Fett had, in fact, made a public appearance nearly two months before the show on a scorching hot day in the streets of San Anselmo, a small Marin County town just north of San Francisco.

An unsuspecting press photographer snapped what is likely the very first public image of the intergalactic bounty hunter, marching alongside Darth Vader before droves of spectators at San Anselmo's Community Fair and Parade on September 24, 1978. The photo was plastered across the front page of *The Marin Independent Journal* the following day. Though the scene-stealing Vader was grand-marshal and consequently grabbed most of the coverage (Boba wasn't even mentioned in the story), the Fett costume must have struck many as exotic, battle-worn, and downright intimidating—which was, of course, the whole point.

"He started as a kind of intergalactic bounty hunter, evolved into a grotesque knight, and as I got deeper into the knight ethos he became more a dark warrior than a mercenary."

– George Lucas

Independent Journal

Even outer space bad guys swelter in Marin

This page: Boba Fett's first appearances, in person and in animation from 1978. Opposite page: Ben Burtt introduces Boba Fett in a Lucasfilm screentest.

COSTUME DESIGN

According to *Once Upon a Galaxy*, the "making of" book for *The Empire Strikes Back*, Boba Fett's character had originally emerged from that of Darth Vader. "I wanted to develop an essentially evil, very frightening character," George Lucas said of Vader. "He started as a kind of intergalactic bounty hunter, evolved into a grotesque knight, and as I got deeper into the knight ethos he became more a dark warrior than a mercenary. I split him up and it was from the early concept of Darth Vader as a bounty hunter that Boba Fett came."

Born of Vader, Fett required an equally villainous look, but something a bit less conspicuous. Designing Fett's signature helmet, armor, and accoutrements fell primarily to Joe Johnston, who worked in tandem with Ralph McQuarrie to come up with the bounty hunter's distinctive look. Far removed from the black-on-black wardrobe of Vader, early concepts for Fett clad the bounty hunter in white, possibly a vestige of his "Super Trooper" origins. This all-white Fett was actually the first costume produced for the character, officially unveiled to Lucasfilm insiders in a screen test shot on June 28, 1978.

In the 20-minute black and white video, sound designer Ben Burtt "hosts" Fett's reveal for Lucas and crew, describing the different weapons, functions, and characteristics of the costume (worn for the test by *Empire*'s assistant film editor Duwayne Dunham, who later directed episodes of TV's *Twin Peaks*). The somewhat amusing footage depicts Fett with a mocked-up laser rifle (which used a lightsaber hilt for the barrel) and a *Star Wars* beach towel doubling as the bounty hunter's tattered serape.

Even at this stage, the plan was to give the costume a muted color scheme, visually placing the character somewhere between the rank-and-file stormtrooper and the fearsome Dark Lord of the Sith. "I painted Boba's outfit and tried to make it look like it was made of different pieces of armor," said Johnston in *Star Wars: The Annotated Screenplays*. "It was a symmetrical design, but I painted it in such a way that it looked like he had scavenged parts and had done some personalizing of his costume; he had little trophies hanging from his belt, and he had little braids of hair, almost like a collection of scalps."

COLORFUL DEBUT

Fett's new color scheme was at least partially
revealed in the *Star Wars* Holiday Special,
which aired on November 17, 1978. Animators
at Nelvana Studios in Canada simplified
the costume's palette a bit by painting the
character it in various shades of blue and green
(a design scheme that was repeated for Fett's
post-trilogy cameo in 1985's *Droids* cartoon
series). The Holiday Special introduced Fett
as a friend of the Rebels, but he was soon
found to be in secret collusion with Darth
Vader. His true colors revealed (in more ways
than one), Fett was now primed to be the next
major villain introduced in *Empire*.

With the Fett out of the bag, the costumed
bounty hunter now took his show on the
road, visiting department stores, malls, and
special events as Vader's enigmatic accomplice.
Like Vader, Fett signed early black and white
photos (as "Boba") and posted "Wanted" flyers
to publicize his role as a bounty hunter, separate
and distinct from a soldier of the Empire.
In the summer of 1979, members of the
Official *Star Wars* Fan Club got a glimpse
of Boba Fett on the back page of the club's
newsletter, *Bantha Tracks*. Describing Fett as
a bounty hunter who "wears part of the
uniform of the Imperial Shocktroopers,
warriors from the olden time," the seeds were
sown to breed rampant speculation about
the origin and identity of the mysterious
mercenary. Continuing the momentum
of pre-*Empire* publicity for the character,
Kenner Products launched its Boba Fett
action figure as part of its second series for
1979. The figure had famously lost its much-
publicized spring-loaded rocket-
firing feature before release, due to
fears of a choking hazard found in a
similar toy line. A 13-inch version of
Fett was released around the same
time, and, like the final costume,
underwent slight modifications to
its paint scheme before going into
production. By the time *Empire*
rolled out to theaters in May, 1980,
fans were well-aware that Fett
would be making an appearance in
the hotly-anticipated sequel. They
may have been surprised, however,
by the small amount of screen time
given to a character that had been talked up
by Lucasfilm for nearly two years. Though Fett
suffered cutbacks in script rewrites, ultimately
the short amount of time he spent on screen
probably helped bolster the mythos that
surrounds him. With so little revealed about
the "galaxy's best bounty hunter," fans were
allowed to fill in the details, making for a much
more evocative and intriguing character. With
the filmed saga now complete, there seems to
be no waning of interest in Boba Fett, whose
character effectively embodies the danger and
mystery found in the darker corners of the *Star
Wars* universe.

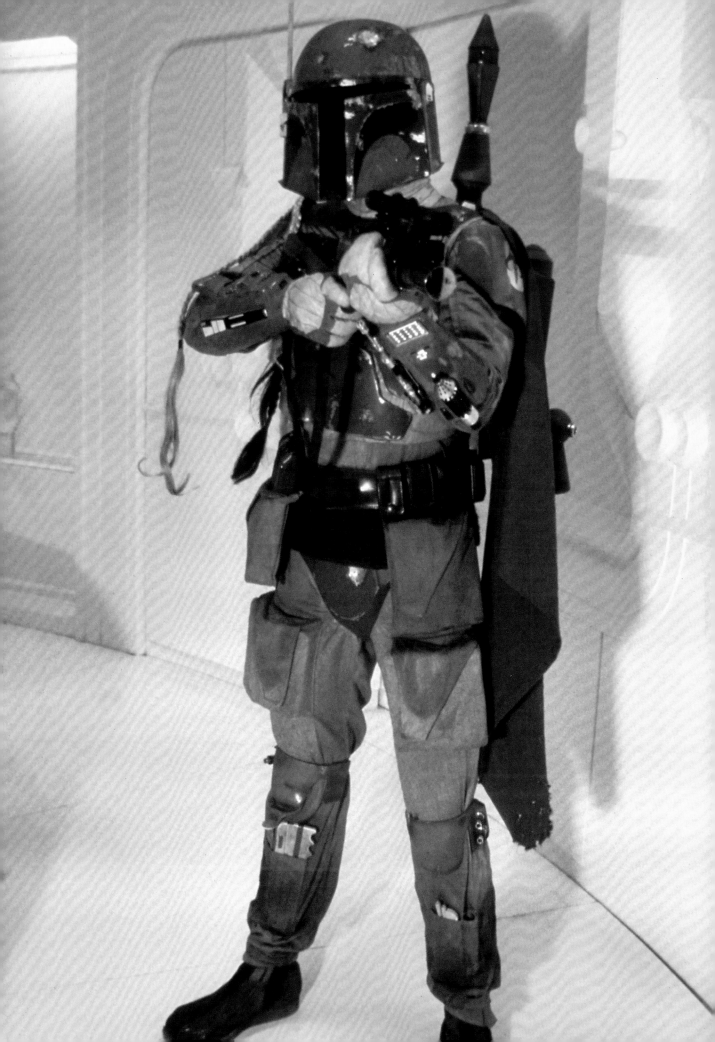

HE'S WORTH A LOT TO ME!

WORDS: NEIL EDWARDS

WHY IT'S A CLASSIC

When he was first introduced in *The Empire Strikes Back* (after an animated appearance in the now infamous *Star Wars Holiday Special* of 1978), Boba Fett had to be one of the most mysterious *Star Wars* characters—a factor that has surely helped make him such a fan favorite over the years.

Little was known about Fett, except that he was a bounty hunter with a fearsome reputation (hence Darth Vader's admonition of, "No disintegrations!" before sending him after the *Millennium Falcon*), and was one of the few characters that could get away with talking back to Vader. Other than that, Fett was a mystery. Was he perhaps the last of a Mandalorian race killed off fighting the Empire or the Jedi Knights? Or was he a stormtrooper deserter who became a bounty hunter? Was there even a man beneath that armor, or was Fett really a droid, or a woman? Only George Lucas knew the answer, and he didn't reveal all until the release of *Attack of the Clones* in 2002.

Designed by concept artists Joe Johnston and Ralph McQuarrie, with armor built by production designer Norman Reynolds' UK art department, Boba Fett was originally screen-tested with his armor all in white as a super stormtrooper. His first public appearance in his painted armor was marching in the San Anselmo Country Fair Parade on September 24, 1978, alongside Darth Vader—he has inspired many cosplayers since.

Given this popularity, it was perhaps no surprise that the Boba Fett action figure quickly became a highly sought-after product. The first mail-away figure for *Empire* in 1979 (before the film was even released), Fett was originally advertised as coming with a rocket-firing jetpack—a feature that was re-thought at the prototype stage due to safety concerns. The few prototype versions with that feature naturally became the Holy Grail of *Star Wars* action figure-collecting. Even Fett himself would be hard pushed to track one down!

The Boba Fett that finally made it to retail may have lacked the ability to fire projectiles, but for all that, it was still a remarkably faithful reproduction of the character, arguably one of the best figure designs at that point. Weapons and accessories such as the wrist-mounted rocket and decorative, braided Wookiee scalps on his shoulder were clearly visible, confirming there was a lot more to the bounty hunter than we even saw on the screen.

The popular figure—with its mysterious markings, battle damage and trophies—encouraged kids' imaginations. Now we could all create Fett's origins and his adventures. That's the beauty of *Star Wars*—even a character who only had a handful of lines could inspire.

ESSENTIAL TRIVIA

One rocket-firing prototype Boba Fett figure sold at auction for $16,000 in 2003, while a still-boxed Boba Fett figure (thought to be one of only a handful in mint condition in existence in the world) sold for the impressive bounty of £18,000 ($27,764) at a UK auction in January 2015.

WHAT THEY SAID

"Boba Fett stayed pretty true to the original design on paper, the ones that Ralph [McQuarrie] and I had done. The character was originally a 'Supertrooper,' all in white like the stormtroopers, but George decided to make him a bounty hunter so I painted the suit up as a multi-colored, beat-up outfit. Loads of fun!"—Joe Johnston, ILM art director, co-designer of Boba Fett, interview with Yahoo! Movies, November 25, 2014

"I designed the final version of Boba Fett. Ralph and I both worked together on preliminary designs, and we traded ideas back and forth. I painted Boba's outfit and tried to make it look like it was made of different pieces of armor. It was a symmetrical design, but I painted it in such a way that it looked like he had scavenged parts and had done some personalizing of his costume; he had little trophies hanging from his belt, and he had little braids of hair, almost like a collection of scalps."—Joe Johnston, ILM art director, co-designer of Boba Fett, *Star Wars: The Annotated Screenplays*, Del Rey Books, 1997

a Fett:
ty Hunter's Journey
[by Leland Y Chee]

THE TANGLED PAST OF BOBA FETT IS A STRIKING EXAMPLE OF JUST HOW MESSY *STAR WARS* EXPANDED UNIVERSE CONTINUITY CAN GET. HIS EARLY LIFE REMAINED A MYSTERY UNTIL THE MID-1990S, WHEN CLUES TO HIS PAST AS A JOURNEYMAN PROTECTOR FROM CONCORD DAWN BECAME HIS OFFICIAL BACK-STORY FOR A TIME. BUT WHEN EPISODE II REVEALED BOBA FETT AS THE UNALTERED CLONE OF A BOUNTY HUNTER NAMED JANGO FETT, HIS PAST HAD TO BE COMPLETELY REWRITTEN. IN CELEBRATION OF BOBA FETT'S APPEARANCE IN *THE CLONE WARS* ANIMATED SERIES, *INSIDER* TAKES A LOOK BACK AT OVER 30 YEARS OF BOBA FETT'S EVER-CHANGING HISTORY.

NOVEMBER 1978

An 11-minute animated segment of *The Star Wars Holiday Special* produced by Nelvana Studios introduced Boba Fett to a nationwide audience, a year and a half before the release of *The Empire Strikes Back*. In that story, he befriended Luke Skywalker only to later reveal himself as an agent of Darth Vader.

1979

Kenner Products announced a mail-away offer for a free Boba Fett action figure. Card backs printed with the description of a rocket-firing Fett were covered up with a sticker that provided hints at Fett's role in the *Star Wars* sequel after the missile-firing feature had to be abandoned for product-safety reasons.

MAY 1980

Boba Fett made his movie debut in *The Empire Strikes Back*. Though he spoke only four lines in the entire film, he immediately entered the pantheon of favorite *Star Wars* characters. Fett made good on the promise of being a threat to Han Solo when he loaded the carbonite-frozen scoundrel into the cargo hold of *Slave I* for delivery to Jabba the Hutt.

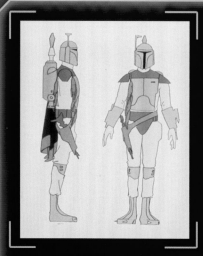

JUNE 1980

STAR.WARS™   By Russ Manning and Don Christensen

Boba Fett made his first appearance in *Star Wars* fiction in the *L.A. Times Syndicate* daily newspaper strip story arc entitled "The Frozen World of Ota," by Russ Manning and Don Christensen. Ignoring the events of the *Holiday Special* cartoon, Luke Skywalker once again met Boba Fett for the first time.

FEBRUARY 1983

A flashback in Marvel Comics' *Star Wars* #68 by David Michelinie linked Boba Fett to the Mandalorian supercommandos who fought in the Clone Wars.

SEPTEMBER 1985

Boba Fett made a second animated television appearance in the *Droids* cartoon episode entitled "Race to the Finish," again produced by Nelvana. In this story, crime lord Sise Fromm hired Fett to hunt down speeder racer Thall Joben. According to official *Star Wars* timelines, the *Droids* series took place before Fett's appearance in the *Holiday Special*, and yet in both stories R2-D2 and C-3PO supposedly met Boba Fett for the very first time.

NOVEMBER 1994

The *Star Wars Galaxy* Series Two Trading Cards featured a card with art by Dan Brereton depicting the artist's interpretation of Boba Fett with white hair, pointed ears, and goatee. Whether this was the official canon version of Fett without the helmet was left open for debate.

BOBA FETT

SPECIES:
Human

SEX:
Male

HAIR COLOR:
Unknown

EYE COLOR:
Unknown

HEIGHT:
1.8 meters

HOMEWORLD:
Unknown

POLITICAL AFFILIATION:
Free-lance bounty hunter

WEAPON(S) OF CHOICE:
Mandalorian battle armor
and various weapons

VEHICLE OF CHOICE:
Kuat System's
Engineering limited-pro
duction, high-speed
Firespray-class ship
Slave I MandalMotors
Pursuer enforcement ship
Slave II

FIRST APPEARANCE:
Star Wars Holiday Special

The Boba Fett entry in the *Essential Guide to Characters* by Andy Mangels was the first attempt to reconcile all of Boba Fett's previous appearances into a single continuity, despite numerous contradictions. The entry revealed for the first time that Boba Fett had been a Journeyman Protector from Concord Dawn. This back-story foreshadowed original material from the upcoming *Star Wars Tales* anthologies that wouldn't be released until 1996.

Tales of the Bounty Hunters "The Last One Standing: The Tale of Boba Fett" by Daniel Keys Moran showed a glimpse of Boba Fett's past life as Jaster Mereel, a man convicted of murder. Mereel would shed his identity to become Boba Fett, though his acquisition of his Mandalorian armor is presented as a mystery, without reference to the Clone Wars flashback suggested in the earlier Marvel Comics. One peculiar scene from that story provides unusual personal insight into Fett's character. When presented with the companionship of the enslaved Princess Leia as a gift from Jabba the Hutt, Fett revealed his views on premarital relations as amoral.

The *Star Wars: A New Hope* and *Return of the Jedi* Special Editions added newly-filmed shots featuring Boba Fett. In *A New Hope*, Boba is with Jabba's retinue in Docking Bay 94 looking for Han Solo. In *Jedi*, a quick shot of Boba Fett flirting with one of Jabba's dancers had fans rethinking Fett's previous views on premarital relations.

Boba Fett featured prominently in the *Shadows of the Empire* multimedia storyline, most notably in the six-issue comic series by John Wagner. These comics focused on Fett's battles with fellow bounty hunters including IG-88, Bossk, 4-LOM, and Zuckuss to claim the bounty on Han Solo.

Rebel Dawn by A. C. Crispin, part three of the Han Solo novel trilogy, featured Fett's early interactions with Solo and Lando Calrissian. Delving deeper into the intertwined pasts of Fett and Solo, Boba was the bearer of bad news, telling Solo of the death of Solo's ex-girlfriend, Shira Brie.

Bounty Hunter Wars #1: *The Mandalorian Armor* by K.W. Jeter featured Boba Fett's involvement in bringing down the Bounty Hunters' Guild. We also learn about one of the more unique partners in Boba Fett's early career—D'harhan, a bounty hunter with a blaster for a head.

In *Boba Fett: Enemy of the Empire* #4, again by John Wagner, the bounty hunter narrowly escaped with his life after facing off against Darth Vader on the planet Maryx Minor.

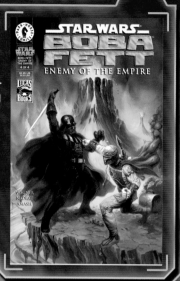

As George Lucas developed the script for *Attack of the Clones*, it became clear that Boba Fett's early EU history would have to be completely overhauled, if not discarded entirely. During the development of the *Star Wars* Bounty Hunter video game and the tie-in comic *Jango Fett: Open Seasons*, the writers at LucasArts came up with a way to pay homage to Boba's previous history while keeping in line with Lucas' vision. It would now be Jango Fett who was born on Concord Dawn. Jaster Mereel would evolve into a separate Mandalorian character who adopted Jango.

Star Wars Underworld #1-5 by Mike Kennedy and Carlo Meglia showed Boba working for Jabba among several teams of scoundrels and bounty hunters, including Han Solo, Lando Calrissian, Greedo, Bossk and Dengar in the search for the Yavin Vassilika. In a strange twist, Fett's role was to protect the competitors.

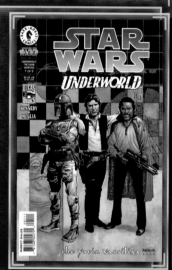

Though originally approved as an *Infinities* story not necessarily a part of the official *Star Wars* canon, "Outbid but Never Outgunned" from *Star Wars Tales* #7 by Beau Smith revealed Boba Fett's relationship with a female bounty hunter named Sintas, with the implication that Boba and Sintas had a child together. An article in *Star Wars Insider* would eventually make Fett's child, named Ailyn Vel, a part of official continuity. Ailyn would later be featured in the novel Legacy of the Force: *Bloodlines*, set 40 years after the events of *A New Hope*.

The Jango Fett and Zam Wesell one-shots by Ron Marz showed glimpses of domestic life on Kamino with young Boba playing with his toys as his father Jango drops by in between bounty hunter missions.

The six-book Boba Fett junior novel series from Scholastic started off with *Boba Fett: The Fight to Survive* by Terry Bison depicting events leading up to and through Episode II *Attack of the Clones*. With Elizabeth Hand penning books 3-6, the series followed the now fatherless Boba and his constant struggles in a galaxy engulfed by the Clone Wars. Plotlines included Boba Fett flying *Slave I* under the tutelage of Aurra Sing, and Fett's ongoing vendetta against Mace Windu. To further complicate matters, Fett harbored one of the galaxy's greatest secrets—that Count Dooku, leader of the Confederacy, was also known as Tyranus, the man who hired Jango to be the host for the clone army.

MAY 2002

The theatrical release of *Attack of the Clones* finally gave us George Lucas's true vision of Boba Fett's past as the clone of Jango Fett, the galaxy's greatest bounty hunter and the template for the Republic's mysterious clone army.

AUGUST 2002

Though *Infinities: The Empire Strikes Back* #2 took a "What If?" approach to *Star Wars* continuity, this was the first post-Episode II appearance of an adult Boba Fett without his helmet. Other licensed products featuring Fett without the helmet included a Boba Fett 3 3/4" action figure from Hasbro and a Boba Fett Mimobot USB drive.

JANUARY 2003

Star Wars Empire #4: "Betrayal" showed Boba coming to the aid of Darth Vader shortly before the events of *A New Hope*, with any past rivalries behind them.

APRIL/MAY 2003

Available through the Scholastic Book Clubs, Episode II Adventures #4: *Jango Fett vs. the Razor Eaters* and Episode II Adventures #5: *The Shape-Shifter Strikes* by Ryder Windham showed Jango and Boba prior to the events of *Attack of the Clones*. The plots pitted the Trandoshan father-son duo of Cradossk and Bossk against the father-son duo of Jango and Boba Fett.

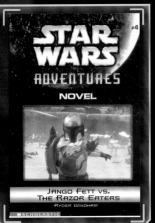

APRIL/JULY 2005

Depicting events between Episodes III and IV, Last of the Jedi #1: *The Desperate Mission* and Last of the Jedi #2: *Dark Warning* by Jude Watson featured Boba Fett and the blaster-headed D'harhan hunting the Jedi.

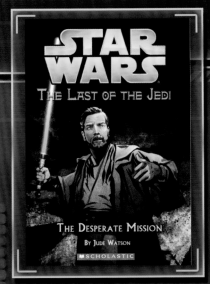

JULY 2009

One piece of Season Two concept art for Boba Fett appeared in *The Art of Star Wars: The Clone Wars* book that debuted at San Diego Comic-Con International in 2009.

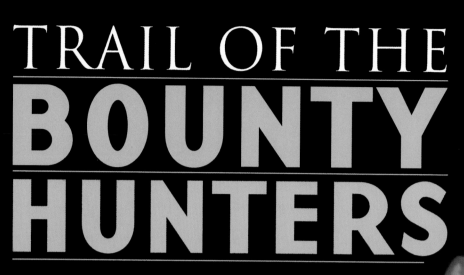

TRAIL OF THE
BOUNTY HUNTERS

ON THE HUNT FOR THE ELUSIVE AND INVENTIVE SCUM OF *THE EMPIRE STRIKES BACK*

BY SCOTT CHERNOFF, WITH RICH HANDLEY

Dengar – a battle-scarred thug with a surly scowl. Zuckuss – his huge insect eyes deflecting attention from well-concealed weaponry. Boba Fett – the eye-catching rogue who somehow knows Darth Vader. Bossk – reptilian and angry. 4-LOM and IG-88 – the first evil droids glimpsed in the saga, programmed to search and destroy. All in all, these guys looked a lot harder to shake than Greedo.

Yet just as quickly as we met them, they vanished without a trace, with only

Boba Fett triumphantly showcased in *Return of the Jedi*. Fittingly, the actor inside the Boba Fett costume, Jeremy Bulloch, has been the most visible of the actors who portrayed *Empire*'s bounty hunters. While his star has steadily risen, the identities of the remaining actors have been as shrouded in mystery as the characters themselves.

When **Star Wars Magazine** embarked on a search to find the previously-uncredited performers behind the bounty hunters for the *Empire Strikes Back* 20th anniversary, we knew it would be tough. What we didn't realize was that the quest would only be fulfilled through the combined efforts of our readers and reporters, Lucasfilm archivists, *Star Wars* saga sound designer Ben Burtt, *Empire* producer Gary Kurtz, and even the ultimate bounty hunter himself – Jeremy Bulloch, who provided crucial assistance in tracking down some of his colleagues.

When the search began, all we had to go on was what Lucasfilm's Steve Sansweet and librarian Jo Donaldson gleaned from an original *Empire* call sheet. Other than Boba Fett, the call sheet didn't have specific character names for the bounty

hunters; instead, they were called Lobster Head, Lizard Head, Human and Insect Head – which we interpreted as, respectively, Zuckuss, Bossk, Dengar and 4-LOM. With no listing for an IG-88 actor, we figured there was nobody inside the droid's tall, thin frame.

Once we had a few actors' names – Cathy Munro for Zuckuss, Moray Bush for Dengar, and Chris Parsons for 4-LOM – we enlisted the help of Jeremy Bulloch, who agreed to join the hunt. Using his connections in the British acting world, Jeremy immediately tracked down Chris Parsons, and using another call sheet, he identified the actor behind Bossk as Alan Harris.

We were also able to find, for the first time ever, the voice of Boba Fett, Jason Wingreen.

on a shelf, original tapes, as well as a contract and record of payment to Wingreen, finally confirming his role in the saga.

"I had fun," super-sleuth Burtt said. "It's always fun to review the different voices and many takes of dialogue which eventually end up getting edited down to one specific and ultimately 'classic' reading of the line. It was an audio reunion of sorts."

Sadly, after an extensive search, we learned of the passing of Moray Bush, whose Dengar made such an impression on fans that he is among the most requested interviews in *Star Wars Magazine* history. It was such a

---

"BOUNTY HUNTERS. WE DON'T NEED THAT SCUM."
Oh, yes we do. Admiral Piett's disdainful dismissal marked the six new characters gathered by Darth Vader in *The Empire Strikes Back* as the riff-raff of the galaxy, a fistful of fierce fighters with allegiances to neither the Empire nor the Rebellion, but only to themselves. They were the bounty hunters, the coolest collection of criminals ever introduced in outer space.

That search was aided by contributor Rich Handley, Elise Cronin and Alan Vasquez of Lucasfilm's legal department, and the actor's proud great nephew Dan Stillman. But the crucial moment came when Ben Burtt and Lucasfilm archivist Sandra Groom located, high

request, from a reader named Warren Johnson, who suggested that Bush was a friend of Darth Vader actor David Prowse, that led to Prowse confirming Bush's passing.

Remaining at large is Zuckuss actress Cathy Munro, for whom we have no information, and the person who performed IG-88. Don't think we didn't look. If you're out there, Cathy and IG, drop us a line! Still, our bounty hunter search introduces three new faces to the *Empire* pantheon, and identifies two more new names. After 20 years, time has finally caught up with the bounty hunters of *The Empire Strikes Back*.
– *Scott Chernoff*

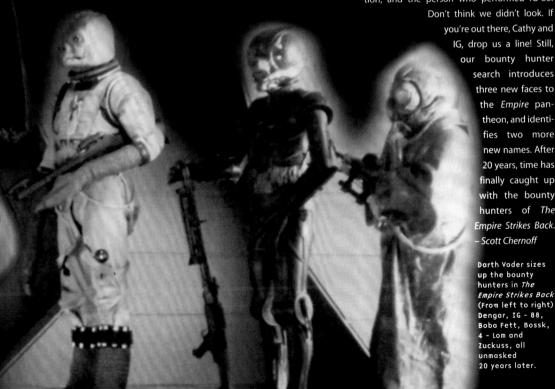

Darth Vader sizes up the bounty hunters in *The Empire Strikes Back*: (From left to right) Dengar, IG-88, Boba Fett, Bossk, 4-Lom and Zuckuss, all unmasked 20 years later.

BOBA FETT:

made for 1978's *Star Wars* Holiday Special) became so popular among *Star Wars* fans that he was not only given a prominent afterlife in the expanded universe of comics and novels, but also added to the *Star Wars Special Edition* and given more screen time in the *Special Edition* of *Jedi*, where he was played by ILM droid operators Don Bies and Nelson Hall. (ILM's Mark Austin played him for *A New Hope*.)

"They were trying to make him a ladies man," Bulloch said of the new footage. "If it had been me, I would have said, 'Can I perhaps grab her by the chin and push her away?' Because he becomes vulnerable. I don't think he would let his guard down. But I was really pleased with the re-release because they put Boba Fett in *Star Wars* as well, just as a presence."

As with Fett's insertion into *A New Hope*, the character's announced appearance in *Star Wars*: Episode II (due in 2002) speaks to the vast following Boba Fett captured, seemingly without trying. The actor said the character's popu-

larity is due largely to all the questions that never get answered during his brief time on screen. "People ask, 'What's that beneath the kneepad? What about those little things in your pockets?' There's so much gadgetry to him - he's a walking arsenal, really."

Carrying that arsenal around the *Empire* set was not easy, the actor recalled. "The costume was very hot, because it was extremely heavy," he said. "And in the carbon freezing chamber, there was steam coming up out of the floor. I was next to David Prowse, and our helmets were taken off every three minutes because it was so hot. We were dripping."

The legendary helmet posed other problems, too. "I remember nearly treading on Darth Vader's cape, coming down the steps into the carbon freezing chamber, because I could hardly see," Bulloch said. "I trod on one of the guys playing an Ugnaught. I trod on his foot, and there was a yelp - I thought it was a real Ugnaught noise. The biggest challenge

Even standing amid the intimidating group of menacing bounty hunters gathered on Darth Vader's Super Star Destroyer, Boba Fett stood out from the pack. It wasn't just that Vader singled him out for a special warning - "No disintegrations." The striking costume, designed by Ralph McQuarrie and Joe Johnston, obviously made an impact, but there was something more mysterious about Fett, something in the way he moved.

"I think the secret to playing Boba Fett - if you can say I played it - is the less you do, the better," said Jeremy Bulloch, the actor who indeed did play the galaxy's most notorious free agent in *The Empire Strikes Back* and again in *Return of the Jedi*. "There is no point in Boba Fett waving his gun around and saying, 'Look at me.' He was very cool, and he didn't move much. I thought of Boba Fett as Clint Eastwood in a suit of armour."

But while Bulloch is quick to give the suit credit for the character's popularity, it's clear from listening to him speak that he put a lot of thought into what could have been a throwaway character but ended up becoming one of the *Star Wars* saga's most enduring - and unexpected - icons.

"Number one, he has respect from people because he captured Han Solo," Bulloch told *Star Wars Magazine*. "He answers Darth Vader back, and he also has a fantastic costume - and I was lucky because I fitted the suit."

Yes, Bulloch clinched the part in *Empire* for precisely that reason. He was invited to audition by his half-brother, *Empire* associate producer Robert Watts. "He said, 'Come see if you fit one of the suits,'" Bulloch recalled. "They were looking for people to fit the costume. Who knows - it could have been a stunt man playing it."

But it couldn't, really - and that's why Bulloch was asked to reprise the role in *Return of the Jedi*. Over the years, Boba Fett (who was actually introduced prior to *Empire* in a cartoon

VOICE OF BOBA FETT:

With barely any lines, and only a few minutes of screen time, Boba Fett became one of the most popular characters in *Star Wars* history. For years, convention-goers have enjoyed appearances by actor Jeremy Bulloch, who gave life to Fett's famous armour, but the identity of the man who spoke those words has remained unknown. Until now. Jason Wingreen, veteran actor of stage and screen, has been confirmed by **Star Wars Magazine** as the voice of Boba Fett in *The Empire Strikes Back*.

Airplane! fans will recognize Wingreen as Dr. Brody of the Mayo Clinic, but he's best known as Archie Bunker's bartender. A native New Yorker, raised in the Howard Beach area of Queens, Wingreen was a natural for the role of Harry Snowden, whom he portrayed for three seasons of *All in the Family* and four seasons of its continuation, *Archie Bunker's Place*. "Before I came out to Hollywood," Wingreen told **Star Wars Magazine**, "I was in a Broadway play called *Fragile Fox*, and I played a character named Private Snowden, so I figured after the war, Snowden became a bartender!"

The actor was amazed to learn how popular his *Empire* work has become with fans - especially since he recorded Fett's dialogue in only 20 minutes. "My agent called me and said to go over to the recording studio, where I met Gary Kurtz and Irvin Kershner," he recalled. "Normally, you see the face of an actor you're dubbing, so you have to lip-synch. But that was no problem here - I could say the lines at any time. I got in position, they ran the film a few times, and I said the lines. Kershner came out and made a suggestion or two and went back in the control room, I did it again, and I was finished."

Wingreen suspects he got the job because they remembered him from an audition for the voice of Yoda. "I was up for it right up to the very end," he said.

was to not fall over, because I was a bit top-heavy with the jet pack."

Still, despite the difficulties, Bulloch managed to stay true to his vision of Fett as High Plains Drifter. "Occasionally, I would make a movement, but a little one, because the less you do, the stronger the character is," he explained. "So I would just stand with my hip one way, and I'd cradle the gun a certain way. He's aware that something could happen any time, so he's quick with the gun. It's ready cocked. He knows exactly what's going on behind him. He may be moving slowly, but he's deadly when it comes to that sudden movement."

During Bulloch's four weeks on the *Empire* set, the actor was also pressed into service for the Empire itself. "One day, I was sitting around in the Boba Fett outfit, and I was asked if I would mind playing this Imperial officer, because there was nobody to play the part. I went into wardrobe, got dressed in an Imperial Officer's uniform, and played this part

who now has a name in the Decipher card game, Lieutenant Sheckil. It was in the scene in Cloud City where Princess Leia says 'Luke, it's a trap' – I drag her away. Moments earlier, you see me as Boba Fett shooting at Mark Hamill."

In the years since *Jedi*, Bulloch has stayed connected with Fett and his fans by becoming one of the most active and in-demand *Star Wars* stars at fan conventions worldwide. "The fans are so polite," he said. "They're amazing. People are always saying, 'Thank you for what you did,' and I always say, 'Don't thank me – thank George Lucas for asking me to do it.'"

Yet Bulloch, 55, is a hero to sci-fi and fantasy fans for more than just the role Lucas gave him. He's also a convention regular for his two *Dr. Who* stories ("The Space Museum" and "The Time Warrior"), his co-starring role as Edward of Wickham in the series *Robin of Sherwood*, and his role as Q's assistant Smithers in two James Bond movies, *Octopussy* and *For Your Eyes Only*. (He also played a different part in an earlier

Bond flick, *The Spy Who Loved Me*.)

Bulloch – the son of a mushroom farmer, a father of three, and now also a grandfather of three – began studying acting at the age of 12, moving from Somerset and Sussex to theatre school in London. "We concentrated on drama, fencing, stage fighting and even ballet – imagine me in a pair of tights," he said.

The training paid off: he's worked steadily in film and television ever since, with other notable projects including the UK soap opera *The Newcomers* and the films *Mary, Queen of Scots* and *Swing Kids*, among many others. He recently appeared in the miniseries *Aristocrats*, is slated to star in an Australian sci-fi film tentatively titled *Master Race*, did a CD-ROM role-playing game with Kenny Baker (R2-D2) and David Prowse, and is awaiting word on *First Frontier*, the sci-fi pilot he made with *Empire*'s Admiral Ozzel, Michael Sheard.

Yet even as Boba Fett, he's still something of an enigma to most moviegoers. "I was having a meal with all the guys after a convention in North Carolina," Bulloch recalled. "A woman asked if we would all sign her menu. So we all signed our names and characters – Darth Vader, Chewbacca, R2-D2, Wicket and me – and gave it back to her. Suddenly I hear this voice behind me say, 'Who the heck is Boba Fett?'

"She knew all the other characters, but Boba Fett, she hadn't a clue. Fans know him, but the general public doesn't. So in a way, it's quite nice, because he is still a mystery." – SC

Jason Wingreen

"He's no good to me dead."

When Lucas wooed Frank Oz to the role, Wingreen accepted Fett's voice instead. But since the film was produced under a British contract and he earned no royalties, Wingreen did not make much money off Fett – until Underoos unveiled its line of *Empire* underwear. "The advertising agency doing the campaign decided they wanted the actor who did the voice to do the promotion," he said, "and the residuals for the commercial were about 20 times what I made doing Fett on film!"

Wingreen, 80, has since retired after a 54-year career and is living comfortably in Studio City, California. "I decided when I was 75 that I'd had enough," he said. "My wife was ill, and after she died, I said, 'I don't need to get up at 4:30 in the morning and trip over the cables anymore.'" His final acting jobs were an episode of *Seinfeld* called "The Opera" and a two-hour episode of *In the Heat of the Night* that reunited him with *All in the Family*'s Carroll O'Connor one last time. Other roles he recalls fondly include the Conductor in the *Twilight Zone* episode "A Stop at Willoughby" and Dr. Linke in the *Star Trek* episode "The Empath."

Wingreen still gets a lot of fan-mail for the role of Linke, and can probably expect a lot more now for Fett. But his favourite role will always be Harry the Bartender. "Playing a character for seven years was a lot of fun," he said. "And it allowed me to retire, too!"
– Rich Handley

BOSSK:

Few actors have worked on all four *Star Wars* films, but British performer Alan Harris is one of them. Harris played numerous roles in the saga, beginning with Leia's Rebel escort on Yavin IV in *A New Hope*. But his most famous role was Bossk, the Trandoshan bounty hunter introduced in *The Empire Strikes Back*.

The character of Bossk, Harris told *Star Wars Magazine*, was created by director Irvin Kershner. "He just put things together," Harris recalled. "I was actually in a very early spacesuit – it looked like one of those old diving-bells they used to go down into the sea. Then they made the head, arms, hands, and feet in the model shop."

The combination made for a memorable look, but moving in the reptilian costume wasn't easy – Harris could only see out of one of Bossk's nostrils. Still, he readily reprised the part in *Return of the Jedi*, when Bossk is briefly glimpsed hanging out with Jabba's gang. In *Empire*, he also played Jerrol Blendin, one of Han's post-freezing Cloud City police escorts. "It was a bit like the first scene in Olivier's *Hamlet*," recalls Harris, "when four guys were carrying his father up onto the parapet of the castle."

Harris was also asked to stand-in for Anthony Daniels as C-3PO. Having been Gene Hackman's stand-in in *Superman: The Movie*, he was experienced reciting lines off-camera so the on-screen actors could time their own dialogue. Like 4-LOM actor Chris Parsons, Harris was Daniels' stand-in on both *Empire* and *Jedi*, making him available for other tasks. For instance, he revealed, "the costume for Boba Fett was made around me because I was the same size as Jeremy Bulloch. I did four fittings over

4-LOM: Chris Parsons

Landing a film role is rarely easy, but sometimes all it takes is fitting the suit. Just ask Chris Parsons, a British actor who at age 18 was called in as an extra on *The Empire Strikes Back*. "I didn't know what the film was about," Parsons told *Star Wars Magazine*, "but it turned out to be the second *Star Wars*, and I was asked to audition for the role of the white 3PO."

The hardest part, said Parsons, was fitting in the 3PO costume. "A couple of guys before me tried out and couldn't handle the face being put on. It was locked with screws and bolts – once it was on, you were stuck until someone took it off. I was told a couple of guys freaked out, but they put it on me and it fit like a glove." Parsons was asked to do "The Walk" created by Anthony Daniels and left with a good feeling about the audition, unaware this would lead to a variety of other roles, including the infamous bounty hunter 4-LOM.

When *Star Wars* first came out, Parsons, then 16, thought it was a children's film and never bothered to see it. But he saw it three times during its 1979 re-release and grew to love it, soon joining the cast as the white protocol droid on Hoth, K-3PO, and as a stand-in and double for Anthony Daniels.

"I was the same height and the same build as Tony," Parsons explained, "so that made it all very easy. We had our own little dressing room on the stage, with a partition between us. It was a very pleasant experience." A permanent fixture on the *Empire* set, Parsons was even approached to hand-model for Mark Hamill while 2-1B adjusted

Luke's bionic hand; unfortunately, he recalled, "my habit of nail-biting precluded my taking the role." Instead, he was asked to don another droid outfit for the bounty hunter scenes, and thus 4-LOM was born.

Still, it was a brief shot, and more memorable to Parsons was his time in the 3PO suits. "I attended *Empire*'s official première as C-3PO," he adds, "then did two or three appearances at events for underprivileged children." He reprised his protocol droid roles for *Return of the Jedi*, then stopped acting to pursue a career in hotel properties, seeking financial stability.

Though 4-LOM has taken on a life all its own in the expanded *Star Wars* universe, to Parsons it was just another role. Stunned to learn of the droid's popularity, he recently ordered a copy of *Tales of the Bounty Hunters* to study 4-LOM's background – and he hopes to begin making convention appearances to share his memories with the many fans he never knew he had. – RH

Alan Harris

about three weeks. The gas jet on his left wrist was practical originally – the effects guys made it a working flame-thrower, but George decided it was too dangerous. Also, it was bloody heavy."

Ironically, Harris had also been a model for Harrison Ford's body-mould for the carbonized Han. "Originally, they made a complete body mould all around me for Harrison, but they decided they wanted something people could carry so they did another one on the floor." Ford's head was then added to the prop to give the illusion that Han was frozen inside.

Now in his 60s, Harris is working "less and less in the film game; I just do extra work when it comes up." His recent work includes *The Winslow Boys*, the upcoming *102 Dalmations* – and *The Phantom Menace*. "I was Terence Stamp's double for Valorum. I stood in for him while he was walking with Queen Amidala, and then they did an effects thing to show the little boy between us as we were talking. Later, when Terry did a speech to the Senate, for some reason they weren't satisfied with something below head-level, so they did me doing the speech and pointing down, then just floated my head off digitally and floated his head on."

Harris described himself as "a worker," and said he loves being an extra. Though he hasn't yet been cast for Episode II, he would love some day to be able to say he was among the few to appear in all six *Star Wars* films. – *RH*

ZUCKUSS: Cathy Munro

The least amount of information is known about the actress who portrayed Gand bounty hunter Zuckuss – which is fitting, because the character of Zuckuss has a history repeatedly marked by confusion.

The licensed *Star Wars* universe contains contradictory accounts of Zuckuss' background, with the character ranging from a lawful, moral and traditional Findsman to an amoral, violent, unorthodox outcast of Gand society. Moreover, when Kenner first released the Zuckuss action figure, its package mistakenly identified the character as 4-LOM, while the droid bounty hunter's package was labeled Zuckuss. This confused collectors who wondered why a droid would have an alien's name and vice versa.

While Lucasfilm's records name Cathy Munro as one of the bounty hunters, no acting guilds count her as a current or former member, making her extremely difficult to track down. In fact, it is unclear as to whether Cathy Munro was her real name or merely a stage-name.

Jeremy Bulloch recalled Munro as having first visited the set because she knew someone involved in the film's production, though he could not recall whom specifically. Alan Harris said she may also have been the actress inside the impolite protocol droid E-3PO, who insulted C-3PO on Bespin with the immortal slur "E Chuta!" Neither assumption has yet been confirmed, but one thing is clear: there is more information readily available about the character Cathy Munro brought to life than about the actress herself. – *RH*

DENGAR: Moray Bush

A bulky frame swathed in layers of cloth and body armour. A bandaged head framing a fleshy face marked by a scowl angry enough to thaw carbonite. A weapon of immense size and heft, dwarfed only by the figure holding it. This was Dengar, a fan favourite among bounty hunters because of his unique back-story: nearly killed in a swoop accident, the cyborg blamed Han Solo for his disfigurement and vowed to avenge himself against his old rival. Beneath the gruff exterior, though, was a man of feelings and passions long forgotten.

British ex-boxer Moray Bush, who reportedly died in the mid-1990s, was the man who brought Dengar to life, and those who worked with him on *The Empire Strikes Back* describe him in remarkably similar terms. "Moray was a lovely fellow," remembered Jeremy Bulloch. "He was a huge man, and he had a big heart." Still, Alan Harris (Bossk) recalled an incident when Bush nearly came to blows with a production assistant over a paycheck discrepancy.

David Prowse, who played Darth Vader in the classic trilogy, worked with Moray Bush on such Hammer horror flicks as *Frankenstein and the Monster From Hell* and *The Horror of Frankenstein*, as well as several other film and television productions. "He was my stand-in on a lot of my work," Prowse told *Star Wars Magazine* "He was a large fellow, like myself, and he always seemed to be there on the same sets I was on." Prowse lost touch with Bush over the years and was saddened to learn of his passing a few years back. "Moray was a great guy," he said. "He was a lot of fun to work with."

Information on the boxer-turned-actor is scant. According to Harris, Bush owned a fish shop in Hastings and worked in films to supplement his income. This, said Harris, is a common trend among British blue-collar workers. While British acting agencies show little record of his film career, one did find evidence of a Mrs. Moray Bush, implying his wife might have acted as well. In addition, Prowse noted that one of Bush's closest friends was Peter Diamond, the stunt coordinator for *Empire*.

Beyond that, Moray Bush's life remains as mysterious as that of the bounty hunter he portrayed 20 years ago. – RH

IG-88: Paul Klein?

H is was the tallest of the original Kenner action figures, a thin assassin drcid with a gun in each hand and glowing red eye-sensors that coldly urveyed their surroundings. One part Terminator, one part f ute, he spoke not a word but transfixed viewers with his mechanical stare.

IG-88 was unique among the six bounty hunters in *The Empire Strikes Back*, for his was the only character not portrayed by a costume-clad actor. Rather, a prop-body situated among the actors was operated remotely to give the illusion of life.

But who was the technician performing IG-88? Lucasfilm has no official record. The only lead was found on the Internet Movie Database (IMDb), which lists a man named Paul Klein as IG-88 (as well as Jabba's palace droids EV-9D9 and BG-J38 in *Return of the Jedi*). But there is no Paul Klein credited on *Empire*'s effects crew. Further, the IMDb is often dependent on unconfirmed information submitted by fans, and *Star Wars Magazine* was unable to determine who submitted the IMDb's IG-88 info. So we don't really know who operated IG-88 – which is exactly how the deadly droid would want it. – RH

The Bounty Hunter Search

If you've got any concrete, substantiated information on Cathy Munro (Zuckuss) or whoever was behind IG-88, please contact *Star Wars Magazine* **immediately! Write to BOUNTY HUNTER SEARCH, c/o** *Star Wars Magazine*, **Titan Magazines, 144 Southwark Street, London, SE1 OUP, or e-mail starwarsmail@titanemail.com and put "BOUNTY HUNTER SEARCH" in the subject heading. You are free to use any methods necessary - but no disintegrations.**

Tsuneo Sanda artwork produced in association with Phil Edgerly Design

BOBA FETT: FROM OBSCURE VILLAIN TO CULTURAL ICON

by Jon Bradley Snyder

Boba Fett is, without a doubt, the most popular supporting character in science fiction history. He is a popularity phenomenon within the popularity phenomena of *Star Wars*. And he's lucrative to boot. If you wanted to measure his onscreen minutes versus licensing dollars generated so far, you would probably find Boba Fett was an investment that rivals Microsoft's initial public offering.

Why exactly is it that this character, who is (supposedly) minor, and (supposedly) evil, and who has not been seen in movie theaters for over 13 years, is still capturing the imagination of fans all over the world? In the films he was portrayed as smart, cunning and tenacious. As a bounty hunter he had a rare talent and he got the job done. During his scant minutes of screen time he was also elusive and enigmatic. Today, in the midst of the second great wave of *Star Wars* spin-off products, the powers-that-be at Lucasfilm have been careful to see that not too much is revealed about him. New novels, comics and games deliberately preserve Boba Fett's air of mystery.

It's not simply the not knowing who Boba Fett is that makes people want to know more about him. The single most interesting aspect of Boba Fett is his outfit. Much credit must be given to Joe Johnston and his design crew. Because of his costume, Boba Fett was one of the most fascinating science fiction characters, even before a line of dialogue was written for him. Like the tattooed-from-head-to-toe Illustrated Man, every aspect of Boba Fett's costume seems to beg a story. If the rocket launcher, the jet pack, the Wookiee pelts, the dented helmet and the flame thrower could all talk, what tales would they tell?

Lately, Fett has been trying to dispatch his greatest enemy: overexposure. Polarity exists within the fan community. Opinions range from "I'm sick of that stupid bounty hunter," to "Why don't you rename your magazine the *Boba Fett Insider?*" In fact some jaded *Star Wars* hipsters have jumped Fett's ship completely, renouncing the king of *Star Wars* cool, and gravitating towards "The Cult of Bib Fortuna," or that of some other obscure *Star Wars* character. While there are still legions of dedicated Fett fans out there, the fact is that Fett's rocketing popularity is now threatening his coolness quotient in the eyes of many old school *Star Wars* aficionados.

Before it all gets out of hand, the *Star Wars Insider* decided to take a long hard look at the fictional entity that Tom Veitch has so affectionately referred to as "The Fett-Meister." Some of the most creative minds in the *Star Wars* universe were gracious enough to offer us their opinions on Boba Fett. We hope you enjoy reading it as much as we enjoyed putting it together.

Dave Dorman
Artist

Of all the characters in the *Star Wars* films, the one character that leaves you wanting more is Boba Fett. I find him interesting because he was important to the plot for the second and third films, yet remained elusive and mysterious because of the lack of background information on him.

I always thought it would have been a great plot twist if it were revealed that the bounty hunter was actually a woman with whom Han Solo had been involved. It would have added a texture and intricacy to Solo's background, and a nice little surprise in the story.

Artistically, I find the design of Boba Fett's costume

intriguing. It provides a great contrast to the costuming of the main characters, which remained black and white or neutral earth tones. Here is an individual that wears a variety of colors, and has a richness of detail in his costume. The addition of curious emblems and insignia on the armor also adds an air of mystery to Boba Fett, and fills the viewer with the urge to learn more about the bounty hunter.

For me, the inventiveness of the costume combined with the enigmatic nature of the character always adds an interesting and fun perspective to the artwork.

Jeremy Bulloch
Actor

Having been an actor for all these years, Boba Fett was just another job to do. For the very first time I was behind a mask. What's extraordinary is that I played Shakespeare's *Hamlet* when I was 19, but I've gotten more recognition by putting a mask on than I ever did from doing that. Which made me wonder; perhaps the best thing you can do is walk around with a mask because you get more recognition by being hidden. With all the really hard work you do with Shakespeare plays, and comedy plays, people say "Oh yes I saw you in that. It was wonderful, but you were *terrific* as Boba Fett." They say this im-

> ## PEOPLE ASK ME: "WERE YOU UPSET THAT YOU ENDED UP IN THE SARLACC PIT IN *RETURN OF THE JEDI*?", AND I SAY, WELL OF COURSE I WAS. I'VE HAD A THEORY OVER THE YEARS THAT HE'S STILL IN THERE, AND OF COURSE HE HAS HIS JETPACK SO HE CAN GET OUT LIKE THEY HAVE DONE IN THE COMICS.
> —**Jeremy Bulloch**

mediately, even people you wouldn't think would be interested in *Star Wars*.

People ask me "Were you upset that you ended up in the Sarlacc pit in *Return of the Jedi*?", and I say, well of course I was. I've had

a theory over the years that he's still in there, and of course he has his jetpack so he can get out like they have done in the comics. But instead he thinks, "It's not too bad down here," and he's decided to open a night club. So with Mrs. Fett, or his girlfriend, he's opened a public sauna, a hotel, and a very nice night

club and he's earning quite a lot of money. He could fly out of the Sarlacc pit if he'd like, but he's actually having quite a nice life, thank you.

Steve Sansweet
Author/Collector

I somehow missed the infamous *Star Wars Holiday Special*, so I was first introduced to Boba as a mail-away Kenner premium. I loved the design of his armor, his missile-firing backpack (rendered useless by product-safety fears) and his unusual ship, the *Slave I*. Even cooler was the 12-inch Boba Fett doll, uh, large action figure, with such add-ons as Wookiee pelts. This was some mean dude, and the copy from Kenner said he was going to be a major character in *The Empire Strikes Back*. So I went to the theater and waited. I can remember that my only disappointment with the film—and a minor one it was—was the fact that Mr. Fett was one of the most minor of characters. Still, he was the ice king, the Colonel of cool. It's the mystery that surrounds him that makes him capable of being just about anything we want him to be.

Steve Perry
Author

"Who Was that Masked Man?"

The Scarlet Pimpernel, Zorro, the Lone Ranger, Ghost Rider, the Shadow, the Spirit, Catwoman, Batman—the list is long and these but a few on it. These are the masked heroes, or anti-heroes, and they have always had a high place in our mythologies. These are the men (and sometimes women) of mystery. These are the enigmas, skulkers in the dark, anonymous doers of deeds, righters of wrongs; the here-be-dragons and don't-tread-on-me kind of folks. Really good...or really bad....

What Makes Them So Appealing?

Could be a lot of reasons, but a big one is that those masks give us lots of room for our own dreams. Shoot, it might be *any*body under there, you can't see his face, after all, so it could be anybody—even you. Maybe *you* could be a dashing character, admired, respected, lusted after, going your own way and living by your own codes. Possessor of a secret identity that allows you to kick butt and take names and devil grab

the stragglers! And if you get tired of it, you can shuck the suit, pull on a T-shirt and jeans and toodle on down to the local cantina to have a brew without anybody being the wiser.

It Does Have a Certain Appeal.

There are many masks in *Star Wars*, from the stormtroopers to Imperial guards, to, of course, the masque o' masques Hisself: Darth Vader. The Dark Lord of the Sith has quite a few admirers of his own. He is tough, powerful, dangerous. It is easy to see why he would have legions of fans.

But Why Boba Fett?

He's a minor character who gets eaten by a toothed hole in the desert early in *Return of the Jedi*. A bounty hunter who says little, does little—he didn't capture Han Solo, after all, Vader *gave* Han to him—and yet Fett is so well-regarded that writers in the *Star Wars* universe have brought him back from the belly of the beast (in the books and stories, at least) and fans can't seem to get enough of him. He's been given a past and a future and life beyond what he's earned on his own.

Maybe it is because Boba Fett is, in his way, even more mysterious than Vader. We know so little about him he becomes a *tabula rasa*, a mostly empty canvas upon which we can paint pretty much whatever we wish. He's a generic anti-hero we can plug ourselves into and go hang out in Jabba's palace drinking the Hutt's hootch and listening to the band as events of galactic importance unfold.

There Are Worse Places to Be.

I've been asked (more than a few times) why there isn't more Boba Fett in the novel *Shadows of the Empire*. He's on the back cover, for chrissake, why don't we get to see him in action? Well, that's simple: he's so popular that even before the folks involved with the *Shadows* project sat down at Skywalker Ranch to carve it into portions, the folks at Dark Horse had already jumped up and laid claim to the bounty hunter, much like your older brother when he yells "Shotgun!" and grabs the front window seat. Like Yoda, calling "Mine! Mine!" Dark Horse snatched Fett away from the rest of us before we could blink.

I didn't really mind—I had Vader, Xizor, the Emperor, as well as Luke, Leia, Chewy and Lando, plus some new characters I got to contribute. So Fett stars in the comics and I think that's where he shines the best. He does, after all, look cool in his T-visor. A man of mystery behind that helmet, shoot, he could be anybody.

Maybe even you...?

Anthony Daniels
Actor

What I like about Boba Fett is that he doesn't interrupt me when I'm speaking. Anyway, a man with a tin head can't be all bad!

Tom Veitch
Author

RETURN OF THE FETT-MEISTER

When we started work on *Dark Empire* in 1988, we knew we could bring back the Emperor, but nobody said anything to us about Boba Fett.

As I worked on the plot I researched fan feelings in Bennington, Vermont, where the *Star Wars* Roleplaying Game was all the rage. Out of those heated discussions, one theme predominated: Bring back Boba Fett.

Encouragement also came from another direction—the artist Cam Kennedy was the world's number one Boba Fett fan. Kennedy's gear-laden warriors, which he began drawing for British comics in the early 1980s, were blood brothers to the Fett. Cam loved the image of a man draped in weapons, ammo belts, leather pouches and lots of mysterious metal junk.

So we put Fett into the script. And Lucasfilm never said no. The bit about the Sarlacc finding Fett "indigestible" was a joke, sort of. We left the explanation for how he actually escaped to the imagination of fandom. (Later Michael Horne constructed a possible scenario for West End's *Dark Empire Sourcebook*.)

Slave I **by Tsuneo Sanda**

BOBA FETT IN PRIME TIME

courtesy of NBC

In case you missed it, Boba Fett got his first sitcom sub-plot on NBC's *News Radio* on the last Sunday in April. *News Radio*, a smart comedy Starring Phil Hartman and Dave Foley, is no stranger to *Star Wars* references (see "Star News: Seen and Heard" issue #29), but this time they really outdid themselves. In episode #219, entitled "Presence," Joey (Joe Rogan) gives Dave (Dave Foley) and Lisa (Maura Tierney) a new Kenner Boba Fett figure with a micro-camera hidden in its head, to help them cheat at a poker game. When they sit down to play, one of the other poker players says "What the hell is that?" "It's Boba Fett, the intergalactic bounty hunter who tracked Han Solo to the cloud city, of huh...Bespin," says Dave his voice trailing off as he realizes he's totally exposed himself as a science fiction nerd. Boba Fett is only seen and mentioned a couple more times on the show, but it's still a momentous occasion. With this episode, Fett is now a certifiable pop culture phenomena, and television is just slightly less of a vast cultural wasteland. The end credits of the show read "Boba Fett courtesy of J.T. Hutt". Look for this *News Radio* in summer re-runs.

Kevin J. Anderson
Author

Boba Fett is the closest thing to a superhero in the *Star Wars* universe, though he always seems to be portrayed in a bad light. Bounty Hunters in general have gotten a bad rap, but Fett is a man of strong character and a rigid adherence to his personal code of honor.

He does not lightly agree to take on a bounty assignment. But once he does he devotes his utmost to the task. Though a man of few words, Boba Fett is smart, resourceful, persistent and always manages to have a trick or two up his sleeve. Perhaps because he has to view the world through a very narrow and rigidly defined slit in his Mandalorian armor, Fett doesn't get easily distracted by irrelevant details.

Han Solo, on the other hand, is the worst sort of bounty, someone Fett would be glad to remove. Not only is Solo a smuggler and a drug runner (hauling glitterstim spice for the gangster Jabba the Hutt), he is unreliable (drops his cargo at the first sign of an Imperial Cruiser), arrogant (sits in a popular cantina when he knows full well there's a price on his head), underhanded (shoots from under the table), a braggart (please don't tell us about that Kessel Run one more time!) and a turncoat (leaves the Imperial academy, breaks the law by being a smuggler, then joins the Rebel Alliance). From Boba Fett's perspective, Solo must be quite a despicable human being! Any reports to the contrary must simply be New Republic propaganda.

Irvin Kershner
Director

It's just a name. He was not important in *Empire*, which I did. And he was not a character I had to deal with. So anything I'd say about him would be secondhand.

Boba Fett seems to be memorable. The name is a good one. George has a way with names. I don't know where he gets them. It was a fun character.

The concept is important. We made him look like he had been through hell. He's not really a character however. Boba Fett is a frightening dramatic element to create tension which puts Han Solo in danger. The concept worked dramatically. The idea of a bounty hunter means someone who will never give up. Also, a bounty hunter has lots of experience. When you think of a bounty hunter you don't think of someone starting out in the business. That's why we made him look like he had been through hell. I guess the look was okay 'cause certainly the dolls have sold.

Then, when the comics were published, fan reaction rolled in, and the audience was clearly divided. Some of the most vehement opinions were voiced on the Fidonet *Star Wars* BBS, where I was a guest for about six months or so, arguing *Star Wars* minutiae.

Opinion seemed to run about 60-40 against Fett's return. I voiced four main arguments why Boba Fett had to live, and I'll give them to you now:

1. We saw Fett fall into the Sarlacc in *ROTJ*, but we never saw him die. The second law of action serials is "If you don't see them die, they are not dead." (Lest we forget, the roots of *Star Wars* are in the Saturday morning serials that Lucas used to watch as a kid.)

2. Too often writers of licensed properties come up with surrogate villains who are only pale copies of the originals. I wanted, wherever possible, to use the adrenaline-charged originals. (I also wanted to use a Vader costume, with somebody new inside it, but they said no to that. But beloved Fett was a go.)

3. Fett disappeared in the films leaving a mystery behind him. Who was he? Where did he come from? Why was he so feared? Where did he get that cool armor? In storytelling you just don't throw away a good mysterious character before his time.

4. Last but not least, I wanted to see Cam Kennedy and Dave Dorman do Boba Fett. That's been my main pleasure in writing comics—seeing how great artists interpret great characters. And these two guys really delivered the goods.

> TO THOSE OF YOU WHO THINK BOBA FETT SHOULD HAVE STAYED IN THE BELLY OF THE BEAST, I CAN ONLY REPLY, LONG LIVE FETT!
>
> —Tom Veitch

Filming Fett in Yuma Arizona for *Jedi*.

To those of you who think Boba Fett should have stayed in the belly of the beast, I can only reply, LONG LIVE FETT!

Kathy Tyers
Author

In *Return of the Jedi*, Boba Fett's silent nod across Jabba's throne room chills me. It's a fangs-bared salute. Another predator brought down the prey he was chasing, then bullied Jabba into accepting terms—and Fett doesn't like it either. He'll be watching Boushh, but for the moment, he acknowledges the catch.

BOBA'S BOUNTY

EVEN BEFORE HIS FIRST SCREEN APPEARANCE, FEARED BOUNTY HUNTER BOBA FETT WAS A FAVORITE WITH COLLECTORS! WORDS & PICTURES: GUS LOPEZ

Despite his rather ignominious apparent demise in *Return of the Jedi*, Boba Fett remains one of the most popular characters of the *Star Wars* saga. He has appeared on so much *Star Wars* merchandise that an outsider might mistakenly think the entire saga is about him. Even before the character's concept was completely nailed down, Boba Fett collectibles were offered to fans who were eagerly awaiting the introduction of this mysterious character in *The Empire Strikes Back*.

(1) One of the first Boba Fett items was a set of lithographs based on early Joe Johnston sketches of the character. The initial concept for Boba Fett was a white-armored soldier, looking not altogether different from stormtroopers. These early lithographs feature the white-clad bounty hunter, with accessories, such as the wrist-activated flamethrower, that would never make it on-screen in the original trilogy but would later surface in Episode II used by his "father" Jango Fett. Acme Archives recently introduced a portfolio containing reduced-size copies of the original lithos.

(2) Ben Cooper, the classic producer of kids' Halloween costumes, created an early version of Boba Fett prior to the release of *The Empire Strikes Back*. The costume, released in Star Wars packaging, had silver on the helmet, foreshadowing Jango Fett's armor over two decades before that character was designed.

(3) For many, the *Star Wars Holiday Special* in November, 1978 was their introduction to Boba Fett. In a 10-minute animated segment that was a highlight of the show, Fett befriends Luke Skywalker while secretly working for the Empire. The *Holiday Special* Fett armor was more colorful than the version in *Empire*, and it would take a couple of decades before Boba Fett appeared in the original *Holiday Special* likeness on merchandise. One brilliantly crafted example was the animated Boba Fett maquette that Gentle Giant made as a *Star Wars* Celebration IV exclusive. With flowing cape and pointed blaster, the piece was a repainted version of Gentle Giant's original Boba Fett maquette. There's even a rare black and white version of the Fett maquette that was only sold in Japan.

(4) In advance of the release of *The Empire Strikes Back*, Kenner Products began promoting the action figure line with its first action figure mail-away offer. A Boba Fett with a rocket-firing feature was heavily marketed on Kenner's *Star Wars* products. However, due to concerns about safety, the rocket-firing feature would never make it to market. Prototypes of the rocket-firing Boba Fett are the quintessential collector's Holy Grail. Although several dozen of these prototypes

are known to exist today, the popularity of the promotion puts it high on the wish lists of many advanced collectors... if they're willing to take out a second mortgage on their homes!

(5) Kenner released a large Boba Fett figure for its *Star Wars* large-size figure line in advance of the release of *The Empire Strikes Back*. The large Fett came with many features and details. Years later, Hasbro released a retro large-size Fett in vintage style packaging, and one of the rare variants of this toy had a blue (instead of gray) body suit.

(6) There's no shortage of novelty Boba Fett items. One of the first *Star Wars* bobbleheads was a Boba Fett Fan Club exclusive that was limited to 4,000 units. Another classic novelty Fett item is the Wilton cake pan. Boba Fett is not only the greatest bounty hunter in the galaxy, he also serves as a fine cake decoration for kids' birthday parties!

Hasbro expanded its *Star Wars* Mr. Potato

Head line to include "Spuda Fett", which became highly sought after... and, perhaps the worst Boba Fett pun ever. Boba Fett also became top-notch character for *Star Wars* Underoos, an honor that not even Han or Chewbacca would get until *Return of the Jedi*.

(7) One of the best likenesses of Boba Fett's helmet appeared in small-scale from Riddell. It was designed by Chris Reiff of SOEDA Inc. Even the paint scheme and scratches closely match those on the helmet first worn by actor Jeremy Bulloch in *Empire*.

(8) Kenner's Power of the Force coin line has been a longtime favorite of *Star Wars* collectors. The Fett coin from that series was never available in stores "on card," and could only be obtained randomly in a mail-away offer that few participated in during the waning years of *Star Wars* interest in the mid 1980s. Thus it is both one of the rarest and also one of the most brilliantly sculpted coins from the line: it shows Fett in front of Jabba's sail barge. There's also a gold-toned version of the Boba Fett coin that was available in stores with the *Droids* series Boba Fett action figure. Rare one-of-a-kind prototypes of this coin include an epoxy hard copy and silicone soft copy that were made six times the scale of the actual coin.

(9) Years later, a Boba Fett medallion was produced for the *Star Wars* Reunion II convention in Paris in 2007. Based on the medallions that had been given away at *Star Wars* Celebration IV, Celebration Europe, and Celebration Japan, artist Mattias Rendahl

based his design on the Kenner action figure standing in front of Cloud City.

(10) The most awesome Boba Fett piece is the life-size statue created by Don Post Studios in the late 1990s. Each detail of Boba Fett's armor and accessories was recreated in this full-scale masterpiece. Production of these hand-made statues was very limited, and there is a wide range of differences in both materials and workmanship. Boba Fett stays cool under fire. ✋

Popular characters of *Star Wars* lore since their first appearance en masse in *The Empire Strikes Back*, the bounty hunters are back with a vengeance in Season Two of *Star Wars: The Clone Wars*. Supervising director Dave Filoni presents the galaxy's newest bad guys!

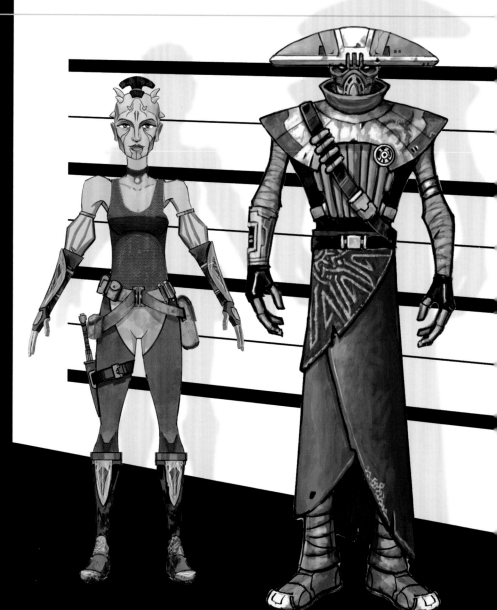

STAR
THE
UNUSUAL SUSPECTS

BOUNTY BUNCH

"When it came to the bounty hunters, we really wanted them to have a lot of colorful elements to their costumes along with different little knives and bits of gear like all the details you see on Boba Fett's outfit. It's great that over the years the fans have decided, 'Oh, those are sonic wrenches,' and other details," Says Dave Filoni. "It might have just been a piece of metal that was shoved in the pocket for effect! We try to make our bounty hunters interesting like that. They definitely have more logos; for some reason there always seems to bea slight NASCAR-effect to the bounty hunters when you see all these emblems. I think that comes from Boba Fett being yellow-shouldered with green armor, and then later having red gauntlets. It makes them stand out. You know instantly they're not Republic or Separatists.

It's fun to pay off that season-opening promise of Rise of the Bounty Hunters, because here come a whole bunch of them!"

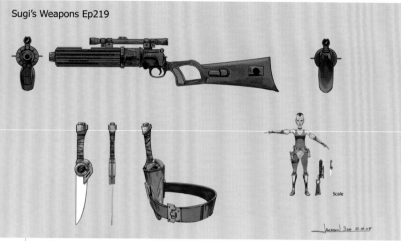

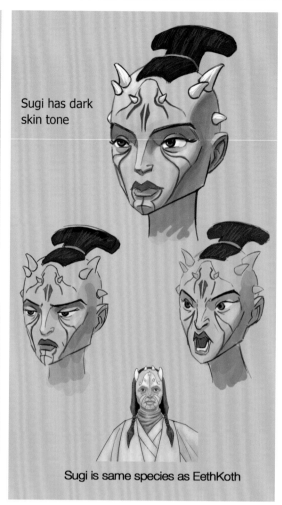

Sugi has dark skin tone

Sugi is same species as EethKoth

SUGI

All Sugi/Sugi weapon illustrations by Jackson Sze.

" She is a Zabrak [the same species as Darth Maul]. We mainly used Eeth Koth as an inspiration for her. There was some debate on whether or not she should have horns. We wondered, do female Zabraks have horns? But let's face it, she's a lot cooler if she has horns than if she doesn't! So since it was never defined, we decided to give her horns. We had a certain way we wanted her shoulders to puff out with a kind of red striping, so there's a little bit of a pirate element to her, with a very specific hairstyle. She really lends herself to being a visually exciting character, but still very human-looking. She turned out to be someone with a really fun attitude. I love the scenes where she's talking with Obi-Wan Kenobi. She seems to stand toe-to-toe with him really well as another very independent, well-spoken being... and she's great with a blaster! "

Sugi Ep219

Sugi production art complete with annotations.

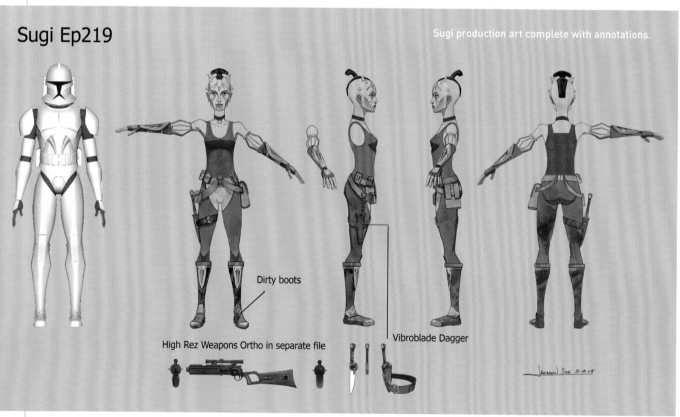

Dirty boots

High Rez Weapons Ortho in separate file

Vibroblade Dagger

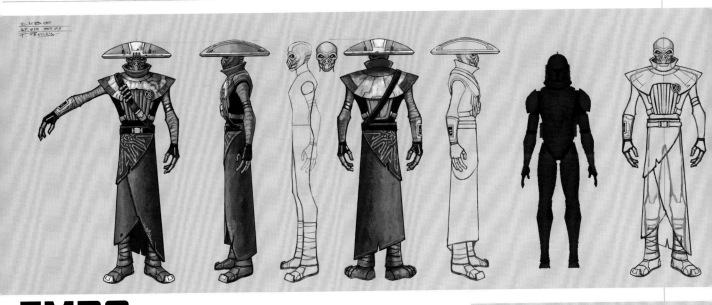

EMBO

All Embo and Embo weapon illustrations by Pat Presley.

> Embo was a design handed to us by George from earlier concept work. We just modified him a bit. He became a favorite character with the team at Lucasfilm Animation. I don't know what it is, maybe it's that hat, but something about him just connected. Steward Lee [the director], and I really wanted to expand what Embo did, as far as action, to show one of these bounty hunters really go to it with their weaponry. Design-wise, there wasn't a lot to develop, because we had such a good head-start from George, but we decided that we wouldn't let him speak English. We just went full-out with an alien tongue that we invented. We don't often do full alien speaking characters in *The Clone Wars*, mainly because of the amount of subtitling that would require—and that's a disappointment. But here we had characters reacting to what Embo says, like they do to R2-D2.

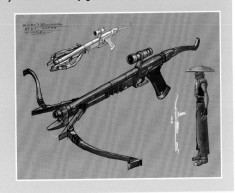

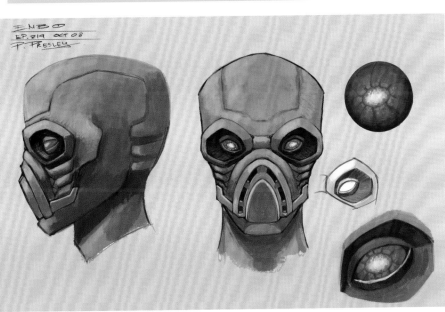

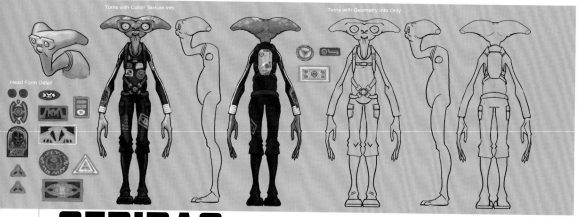

Head Form Detail

Turns with Color/ Texture Info

Turns with Geometry Info Only

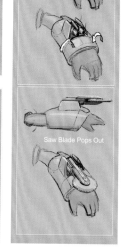

Twin blasters Pop out

Saw Blade Pops Out

SERIPAS

All Seripas images
by Wayne Lo

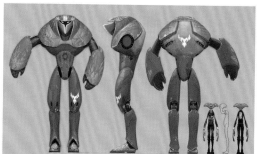

" This was another design that came to us
from George. He is basically a big suit of armor and
George wanted this little guy inside him. Wayne Lo
[the design artist] did this breakdown for him, which
is the exploded view drawing of Seripas that just
looks like a Japanese toy. I loved the way it would
open up. We wanted to have a lot of little colored
lights and stuff inside so we could really see these
lights on his face when he's inside the big suit
of armor. He turned out very cool, but he had a much
more expanded role at one point that we had to cut
down for time. We have these cool bounty hunters
and some of them don't get to do a lot. Once I saw
him without the armor on, I wanted him to have a lot
of patches on his flight suit. And one of the patches
I asked Wayne to include is the *Star Wars* fan club
patch of Darth Vader. So if you look closely, you'll
see this little patch that looks a little bit like a
Vader helmet. It's that one that he's wearing
on his uniform! "

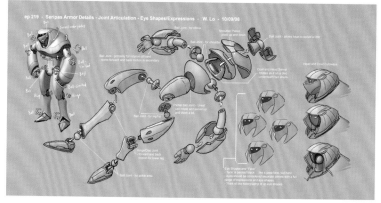

ep 219 - Seripas Armor Details - Joint Articulation - Eye Shapes/Expressions - W. Lo - 10/09/08

ep 219 - Seripas Armor - Cockpit Details and Mechanics - W. Lo - 10/15/2008

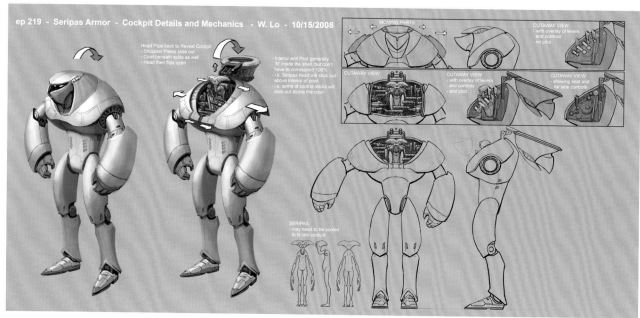

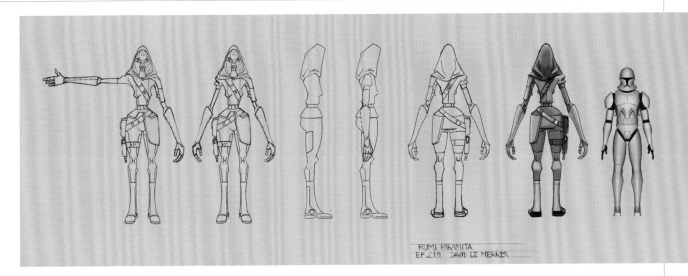

RUMI PARAMITA
EP 219 DAVID LE MERRER

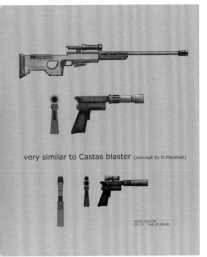

very similar to Castas blaster (concept by D.Marshall)

RUMI PARAMITA

All Rumi and Rumi weapon images by David Le Merrer

"George will often send us a design and say, "I want it to look something like this." Then we have to take it and bring it into *The Clone Wars* world, and sometimes it changes a lot and sometimes it doesn't. But we had a great start with Rumi. She started as a very small mouse, very narrow, which guided how we were going to have the voice acting done. She's just a very bizarre, classic type of alien, with a large head and thin limbs."

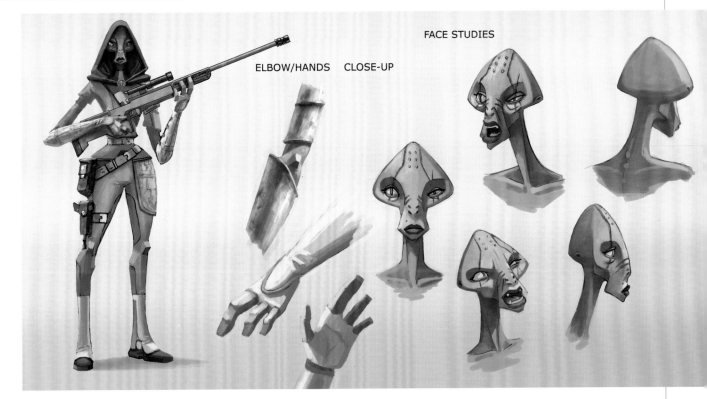

FACE STUDIES

ELBOW/HANDS   CLOSE-UP

SET PIECE

WORDS: CHRIS TREVAS

KAMINO LANDING PLATFORM
DUEL IN A DOWNPOUR

When George Lucas and crew arrived at Stage 1 a day early to film on the Kamino landing platform set, they found it wet—not with rain but with paint that had not yet dried. The main soundstage at Fox Studios, Australia, was so huge they couldn't bring in heaters big enough to raise the temperature and dry the paint quickly!

Once the set was dry however, it could easily be drenched again, thanks to a special rain system, installed by the special effects engineers, led by special effects supervisor Dave Young. Installed in the ceiling and covering the entire platform, square sections could be turned on and off in isolation, to keep the actors wet while the cameramen remained dry. The spray could also be adjusted from large droplets all the way down to a light mist and at a variety of speeds. Water was pumped into the rain system at a speed of seven and a half tons of water per minute, and covered an area of approximately one-third of an acre. To prevent flooding of the entire stage, an 18-inch dam was constructed around the set.

It is on this rain-soaked platform that Obi-Wan Kenobi catches up to Jango Fett and attempts to detain him. He draws his lightsaber quickly, and the bounty hunter opens fire in return. After several exchanges, the two manage to disarm each other and the fight turns from a duel of weapons into an old-fashioned exchange of blows. Punches, kicks, and even a headbutt make this an unusually physical encounter. Lucas filmed for a day with Ewan McGregor and Temuera Morrison capturing most of the close-up action before

handing the reins over to second-unit director Ben Burtt and the actors' stunt doubles.

Morrison recalls being very glad to hand over his helmet. "I'd breathe and it would fog up and I couldn't see anything. I also couldn't hear anything inside it, so I'd be standing there, wondering if they'd said 'action' or not." When the stunt double arrived he told him, "Here, mate. Here's my helmet. You stick this on and go get wet for two days!" The stuntman standing in for Morrison suited up in softer armor made from injected foam for a wider range of motion and to prevent injuries from its hard edges.

Stunt coordinator and swordmaster Nick Gillard choreographed the fight after studying storyboards and animatics prepared by the art department. These computer animations laid out the broad actions needed, and the camera angles, to create an invaluable visual guide for the crew. They portrayed a knock-down, drag-out fight that went beyond what could be achieved on set. Rather than resort to complex wire harnesses or other stunt rigging, the more elaborate acrobatics (and the physically impossible, such as Jango's flying), were left for ILM to execute with digital stunt doubles.

The crew spent a total of four days on this set, filming Obi-Wan's arrival as well as the duel. During post-production, ILM added several computer-generated scenes, but Lucas found he still needed more live action footage than they had been able to capture during the short time in Sydney. Additional pick-up shoots with McGregor and Morrison took place in March 2001, at Ealing Studios in London.

SET DESIGN

Wind machines were scarce in Sydney, Australia, so the crew ended up building their own from scratch in only four days.

SET DESIGN

The platform was only a partial set consisting of less than half of the full circle and not much beyond the edge railing. Surrounding it was a green screen to be filled in with computer generated extensions in post-production.

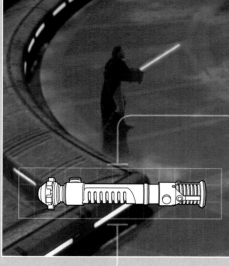

ART

Obi-Wan's lightsaber is a shinier version of the one he lost during his duel with Darth Maul. The props thrown around in this fight were lightweight chromed castings of the original metal prop used in *The Phantom Menace*.

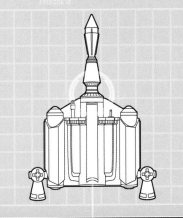

JANGO FETT

Initially, Jango Fett's armor was going to be white as a visual reminder that he is the forefather of the Imperial stormtroopers. When Lucas saw the armor in development, cast in fiberglass and combined with aluminum powder, he decided to leave it the bare metal color.

ART

Jango's jetpack is the exact same design and color scheme as the one worn by his son Boba in *Return of the Jedi*. Since the pack flies off and explodes during this fight Boba must inherit his father's spare.

SLAVE I

Slave I was represented by a simple green ramp on stage. It was there for Boba and Jango to walk up. It was ultimately replaced by a completely computer-generated model ship. The only portion physically built at full-size was the cockpit interior, located on a separate soundstage.

SET DESIGN

Stage 1 was chosen for the Kamino set because the soundstage was sloped for easy drainage. It had originally been built to accommodate livestock (the site was once a fairground), and would have been hosed down regularly.

STUNTS

Lucas pushed the limits of digital stunt doubles in *Attack of the Clones*. He wanted to be able to show them from as close as the knees up, which necessitated more realistic clothing, hair, and skin than ILM had ever done before. This shot of Obi-Wan is a digital double of Ewan McGregor.

IT'S STILL NOT EASY
BEING GREEDO
MEET PAUL BLAKE, THE OTHER GREEDO

by Matt Yeo

[A note from your managing editor] *Ah, the elusive Rodian. In Star Wars Insider #37, I profiled Maria de Aragon, the actress under the mask of the infamous bounty hunter Greedo.*

But imagine my surprise and confusion when I opened the magazine and—right above Maria's quote that she and Harrison Ford never met and were never on the set at the same time—there was a photo of Greedo and Han Solo together, in a shot from their famous and controversial cantina confrontation. Clearly I'd missed something.

That 'something' was uncredited actor Paul Blake, who played Greedo on the British Star Wars set, while Maria de Aragon donned the Rodian mask for pick-up shoots in California. Now, thanks to intrepid reporter Matt Yeo, who writes for our sister publication in the UK, the full story of Greedo can finally be told. Here then, recorded for generations to come, is that story. —Scott Chernoff

Up until now, actor Paul Blake has received no formal credit for playing the ruthless, Rodian bounty hunter Greedo in *Star Wars*—and appearing as another Rodian in the *Star Wars Special Edition*.

For over 20 years, the identity of the actor behind Greedo, the green alien who corners Han Solo in the Mos Eisley cantina, has

ater company with the likes of [comedian/actor] Billy Connolly. I then decided to opt for acting full time and moved to London. I joined the Bubble Theater Company and performed plays and shows written by Spike Milligan and other talented types. From there it was a straight route to television and, eventually, film."

the film's basic story. In fact, I remember that even back then he had a series of nine films planned out and was filming the middle trilogy first. I asked him what character he wanted me to play and he told me about this green-skinned monster. Greedo didn't have a name at the time and was just referred to in the script as 'Alien.' The next day, I went along to the studio to have a prosthetic mask and hands fitted, which was a very strange experience.

"I still wasn't sure about the role, but my first day on the set soon changed all that. The cantina set was there and filled with incredible aliens, most of which you don't actually get to see much of on screen."

Blake's memory of the bar scene is surprisingly vivid. "The cantina booth sections were extremely restricted, so my movements were quite stiff," he recalled. "I remember thinking that the character of Greedo was quite reptilian looking, so I thought about how croc-

"I REMEMBER THINKING THAT THE CHARACTER OF GREEDO WAS QUITE REPTILIAN LOOKING, SO I THOUGHT ABOUT HOW CROCODILES AND ALLIGATORS MOVED WHEN I PERFORMED."

remained a mystery. But we can now reveal that Greedo was played by not one but two actors, each working on either side of the Atlantic. For Paul Blake, the first to wear the green mask (during the original cantina shoot at Elstree Studios in 1976), *Star Wars* was the latest highlight in a diverse career.

"I didn't actually set out to become an actor," Blake said, "but I always enjoyed going to the movies as a kid. I first took to the stage in a band with two other guys and we sang close harmonies. I was only 12 at the time and wasn't very good, but I thought 'Hey, this is showbiz!' I studied English and drama in the '60s in Birmingham. I eventually ended up going to Glasgow for a few years and worked in a the-

But Blake was frank about what he considers the highlight of his career to date. "Well, I'd have to say *Star Wars* really!" he declared. "I'd worked on other movies before, such as a James Bond spoof called *008, Hennessey* with Rod Steiger and *Second Victory*, a World War II film with Max von Sydow, but *Star Wars* was something else altogether.

"At the time," he continued, "I was doing a children's show, *Jackanory*, and a friend of mine, Anthony Daniels [C-3PO], rang me up and said 'I'm doing this sci-fi movie—do you want to be in it?' I thought it might be worthwhile, so a few days later I was at Elstree Studios talking to George Lucas in front of the *Millennium Falcon*! We chatted and he told me

odiles and alligators moved when I performed. The script was also such fun that I almost played the role in a Raymond Chandler detective novel sort of way, even though all my dialogue was dubbed over later. I mean this wasn't *Macbeth* we were doing, but we did work on the dialogue."

The filming of the shoot-out with Han Solo proved memorable, and not a little hazardous. "At one point I was replaced with a dummy filled with explosives," Blake explained. "A hole was drilled through the table, which was fitted with an electronic charge that blew up the Greedo dummy. The special effects guys then ripped the costume off the dummy and dressed me in it again. I couldn't breathe

"JABBA WAS MY BOSS AND WE WERE GIVING HAN SOLO A HARD TIME IN THE HANGAR BAY. BASICALLY, I GOT TO PLAY COWBOYS AND INDIANS WITH A PLASTIC GUN YET AGAIN!"

because they were spraying it with acid to keep it smoking. I nearly suffocated!"

Blake also played the Greedo lookalike Rodian first seen in the Jabba the Hutt footage restored for the *Star Wars Special Edition*. "In the scenes with Jabba the Hutt, played by a fine Irish actor, Declan Mulholland, we filmed about eight hours worth of material," he revealed. "Jabba was my boss and we were giving Han Solo a hard time in the hangar bay. Basically, I got to play cowboys and Indians with a plastic gun yet again!"

Blake's memories of George Lucas broadly concur with other actors' recollections of his laid-back directorial style. "I remember his role as being very much sitting in the background and watching things going on around him," Blake said. "He was a very hands-off director, but it was his vision that impressed me the most. He knew from the start how he wanted things to look and turn out."

Greedo's run-in with Han Solo was one of the scenes that received extra attention in the *Star Wars Special Edition*. In the new version of the film it is Greedo, not Han Solo, who shoots first at the climax of their confrontation. Does Blake feel the scene now works as well as it did?

"Not really," he confessed. "I liked the idea that Solo was portrayed as a cold-blooded killer because that was how the scenario was originally created. It was quite obvious that there were some unsavory characters in that bar and what drew me to that role was that it was very much a shoot-first-ask-questions-later kind of scene. I can see why George Lucas may have wanted to satisfy some sense of morality, but Solo did what he did for self-preservation, which was obviously in keeping with his character. Then again, I guess it does show that Greedo wasn't quite as stupid as he appeared to be."

Actress Maria de Aragon, who also played Greedo, has mentioned that she played the character in later additional filming, and never met Harrison Ford. Had Blake been aware of this?

"The first I heard about this was from a friend of mine on the Internet. He'd seen an interview with Maria and thought it strange as he knew I played Greedo in *Star Wars*. What happened is that I was filmed during the scenes where Greedo is seen walking around and threatening Han Solo. Maria's scenes were obviously pick-ups that were filmed later. The mask I wore had none of the ear or snout movements you see in the movie, so they obviously added that later. I just wanted to set the record straight and make people aware of who else was involved in Greedo's performance.

"In fact," Blake concluded, "for a supposed minor character, Greedo was really a two person job!" ☢

A version of this article originally appeared in our United Kingdom counterpart, *Star Wars: The Official Magazine*.

Got a favorite SUPPORTING *Star Wars* actor you've never seen interviewed? Email your suggestions to Scott Chernoff in the *Star Wars* universe: SWuniverse@aol.com.

[TOP] Greedo (Paul Blake) shoots first in the *Star Wars Special Edition*; [BOTTOM LEFT] A rogue Rodian (Blake) turns his back on Boba Fett in footage restored and enhanced for the *Special Edition*; [BOTTOM RIGHT] Paul Blake unmasked.

After the Elstree shoot for Star Wars came to end, George Lucas convened a smaller crew for various pick-up shots in the United States. Lucas decided the cantina scenes needed special attention, adding the now famous band, and enhancing the prosthetics used for Greedo. Scott Chernoff picks up the story with Greedo Mark II, Maria de Aragon...

Warning to celebrities and other assorted Los Angeles VIPs: the next time you step into your luxurious limousine, watch out for the driver.

She may seem sweet, and chances are she will get you to your destination, but don't be fooled. You may have entrusted your transportation to one of the most notorious bounty hunters in the galaxy.

That's right, Maria de Aragon – the second actor to play Greedo in *Star Wars* – is a chauffeur. "I'm driving the superstars now and having a good time," de Aragon says, adding that most of her film star passengers have no idea their driver appeared in one of the most successful films of all time.

"I've been quiet about it," she admits, "but once in a while I'd mention that I played Greedo and I'd see this huge reaction." It's a good thing she was behind the wheel, de Aragon adds, since things can get dangerous when she reveals her secret while riding in others' cars. "They would practically have an accident. They would stop the car and say, 'You played Greedo? You can't be serious!'"

But de Aragon is plenty serious when it comes to her affection for the Rodian. She (along with sound designer Ben Burtt, who created Greedo's distinctive voice) helped to make one of the most memorable creatures in the cantina. "I love the film," she gushes. "I love the scene I was in, although it's a short one. It was great to be directed by George Lucas, who's so creative and inventive. I hope I have another great director like that some day."

The actress might just get her wish, since she said her two days on the *Star Wars* set in 1976 were, literally, the answer to her prayers. "I had asked the Good Lord above to put me in a film that would have some meaning, and He did," she remembers. "I told Him I didn't care how I looked – and He apparently didn't either."

But 22 years ago, when she was first cast in *Star Wars*, de Aragon had no idea her prayers had been fulfilled. "I didn't realise it would be the huge movie it turned out to be, going down in history like *Gone With the Wind*," she says. "I wanted to be a part of a movie that would be that big, that important to the world. *Star Wars* is exceptional in every way."

A native of Montreal, Canada (she still speaks with a French accent), de Aragon moved to LA 30 years ago, finding work as one of the first female chauffeurs in Los Angeles while building her acting career. "I did a film called *The Cremators* for Roger Corman," she says. "I did *Wonder Women* in the Philippines for Arthur Marx, and another one called *Blood Mania*, a horror film in the Seventies that's still well known at the video stores."

Bar

But while there are plenty of titles on her *resumé* that may not sound familiar (*Teddy Bear Killers*, *Nightmare in the Sun*, *Love Me Like I Do*), there is one that soars right off the page: *Star Wars*. "A friend of mine, George E Mather, was working for industrial Light & Magic [as production supervisor for *Star Wars*]," de Aragon recalls, "and he asked me if I'd be interested in doing a bit part."

That "bit part" was not originally Greedo. "C-3PO [Anthony Daniels] was missing a couple of coverage days, and I was going to do that," she says. De Aragon explains that, although most of the film had already been shot in London and Tunisia, there was still some work left to do in LA, and she was scheduled to fill in as Threepio on the days Anthony Daniels couldn't be on the set.

"I started studying his mannerisms and trying the suit on," de Aragon continued. But on the day she was to make her droid debut, the shoot was cancelled because Mark Hamill also had a conflict. When the scenes were rescheduled, Daniels was available to play C-3PO, and de Aragon was no longer needed.

"A week or so after, I was called and they asked me to come in for a fitting of the green monster – I think that's what they called it at the time. That's how I came to play Greedo, and I'm very happy to have done so."

De Aragon recalled her brief stint on the *Star Wars* set – surrounded by her fellow soon-to-be-

Far left: Maria de Aragon – celebrity chauffeur and part-time intergalactic bounty hunter.

Right: In California in 1976, George Lucas helps a costumed Maria during the filming of the pick-up shots for the Star Wars *cantina scenes. Note Maria's shoes.*

"I was out of oxygen and I couldn't breathe very well ... I had a very bad three, four minutes there."

famous cantina creatures – blissfully. "I remember every monster," she says. "I knew this was not done overnight. It had a lot of thinking behind it. The bar itself was quite a set."

Still, there was one incident she'd rather forget. "It was hot under the mask, and I almost lost my life because I was out of breath. I was out of oxygen and I couldn't breathe very well. I started to make gestures that were out of the ordinary, and George Lucas noticed and made sure I got help. I had a very bad three, four minutes there."

One person not there to help was Harrison Ford. Despite his presence in de Aragon's famous scene – in which Greedo attempts to kill Solo over his debt to Jabba the Hutt (and which aroused some controversy when it was altered in the *Star Wars Special Edition*) – Ford was never on the set with her. "I didn't work with him," de Aragon says. "It was all shot separately. A lot of people don't seem to realise that a lot of shooting is done that way. So no, I did not have the pleasure to meet Mr Ford – although he got the pleasure of killing me!"

De Aragon said Greedo's undignified demise was no surprise. "Greedo was a young monster and very, very cocky," she said. "He probably was a little too threatening too quickly."

Creating that cockiness from beneath the striking and memorable Greedo mask was her primary challenge. "You definitely have to make your body language as threatening as you can," she said, "although when you're sitting down you're slightly limited." The actress admitted she got more than a little help from her incredible costume and voice effects, adding, "Once you see the monster and you look at his gestures, you don't need too much more after that."

Neither, it seems, does Maria de Aragon, whose prayers were answered more than 20 years ago. Still, she does have one more *Star Wars* wish: "I hope," she said, "they keep making them." ∎

DOWN UNDER

AUSTRALIAN ACTRESS LEEANNA WALSMAN
IN STAR WARS: EPISODE II

BY MICHAEL G. RYAN

A YEAR AFTER finishing work on a Fox Studios Australia soundstage, Australian-born actress Leeanna Walsman is preparing for a visit to Industrial Light & Magic in California. There she'll do a little follow-up work for her scenes in *Star Wars*: Episode II *Attack of the Clones*, in which she plays bounty hunter Zam Wesell, who mixes it up with Obi-Wan Kenobi and his apprentice, Anakin Skywalker. That subsequent experience continues to amaze her long after her time on the film's set concluded. *Star Wars Magazine* recently called Walsman at her home in Australia, where the 17-hour time difference made an evening interview in Seattle a mid-morning break for Walsman.

"It's so big," she says of the galaxy in which she plays a character that she refers to simply as "a baddie." "Everybody knows about the film. It's not like I've said, 'I'm doing this little film over here.' Instead, I say, 'I'm doing *Star Wars*,' and people are stunned. They can't believe it. Everyone already knows all about that universe, and everyone appreciates it."

Walsman joins an elite group of actors and actresses who've brought nefarious characters to life in the *Star Wars* galaxy, villains like Darth Vader, Darth Maul, and Boba Fett.

WORLD

ARMS HERSELF TO PLAY A BOUNTY HUNTER

TTACK OF THE CLONES

HUNTING FOR THE PERFECT PART

"All my training up to now has been practical," Walsman says, reflecting on the five years preceding her role in *Star Wars*. "Working. That's where I learned my craft."

Beginning in a small drama troupe in high school, she began to shift her focus from being in entertainment in general ("I thought I wanted to be in a cabaret," the 21-year-old recalls) to acting in particular. As a child, she was particularly inspired by the old black-and-white movies she saw on the big screen.

"I used to have this little old English lady who looked after me named Mrs. Hollyhead – she was so cute! – and every Saturday, she'd take me to the midday movies," Walsman remembers. "All the old classics, the old Bing Crosby or Greta Garbo films. The singing, the dancing, the beautiful women . . . I used to think, 'I want to be just like them when I grow up.' I fell in love with the movies then."

In 1996, Walsman took on her first movie role in an Australian film called *Blackrock*, only to find much of her part on the cutting room floor. "When the film

ZAM WESELL

"What do you mean, 'Exact change only.'?" Bounty hunter Zam
Wesell (Leeanna Walsman) takes aim from the cockpit of her
speeder. Photo by Lisa Tomasetti.

came out, a lot of us weren't in it as much we were supposed to be," she laughs. But the experience not only introduced her to other young actors and actresses with whom she's still friends today, it also led her to an agent via *Blackrock*'s director Steven Vidler, an actor himself. "It was an amazing experience that let me do so much more work," she says.

Since then, Walsman has moved easily among film, television and stage roles, though she says she's not drawn to any particular kind of part. "Actually, they seem to draw themselves to me," she says. "A lot of baddies. Strong characters, I think . . . or else completely emotionally unstable, I don't know which." And in the aftermath of her *Star Wars* experience, she finds herself leaning toward film over other media. "You can see the outcome with film," she notes. "You see a collaboration of ideas all put together. And when you watch it all put together, it's even more different than it was when you were doing it in the first place. It's a whole other world that reaches thousands, even millions, of people. And it's also permanent, like a library. Films can be kept and watched again and again."

Despite her preference for film, Walsman says she owes a debt to theatre, as her participation in *La Dispute*, a dark production by 16th-century French playwright Mariveau, opened up a door to a galaxy far, far away. "Theatre is incredible," she says. "I get fed up with it at times because it's so exhausting, such hard work, but when I don't do it, I miss it. My best work has most definitely been onstage, and I've been able to play a lot of roles in theatre that I haven't yet played in film or on television. It's really beautiful when somebody comes up to you who's never seen theatre before, and they tell you they've been changed by it. You perform right in front of them; you can sometimes even hear what they're saying about your performance, right there. It's so personal."

La Dispute, directed by Benedict Andrews (with whom Walsman has worked many times in the past, and who is currently directing her in *Old*

Masters for the Sydney Theatre Company), stands as Walsman's favourite role prior to her work as a bounty hunter. "The play's about a prince and his princess who have an argument about which sex was the first to be unfaithful. So this man goes out and gets four babies – two girls, two boys – and

THE PRICE OF
"I'VE GOT TO HAVE A LITTLE FIGURINE

"I've got to have a little figurine of me!" Leeanna Walsman says, thinking ahead to when action figures of her character Zam Wesell might appear in toy stores around the world. "Imagine that – a figurine of me! I love *Star Wars*! This has all been so good for me and for the acting community in Australia."

As the film gets closer to release, Zam Wesell will pop up in comics and novelizations. And as fans learn more about the mysterious bounty hunter, Leeanna Walsman might might find herself more and more in the spotlight. Much of the

puts each of them in isolation to conduct an experiment later on. So, 20 years later, his son is having the same argument with his princess, and he says, 'Well, my father did this 20 years ago. Why don't we unleash them and see what happens?' So they release them, and it's very voyeuristic – the prince and princess are staring down at them, the audience is staring in at them, and they're almost like caged animals."

The four caged people – including Walsman's character, Egle – are released into a dirty, zoo-like enclosure for observation. The entire stage is covered with dirt, a stream runs across it, and monkey bars hang overhead. The four subjects of "the dispute" are amazed by what they encounter here for the very first time: each other. Jealousy, vanity, and numerous other previously suppressed emotions come boiling out of the four characters, who behave like animals as they climb the monkey bars, dive down slippery slides amid the dirt and water, and tumble over one another, exploring their new world.

"Robin Gurland, who was casting *Star Wars* in Sydney at the time, came to see the play," Walsman says. Gurland had come to see Rose Byrne, who played the second female lead in *La Dispute* and who was ultimately cast as a handmaiden in Episode II. What Gurland saw in Leeanna led to her offer to do *Star Wars*.

While the play brought about a happy turn of events for Walsman personally, *La Dispute* itself

FAME
F ME!"

ripple effect of being in such a huge film hasn't quite registered on her yet, as she contemplates attending a premiere of the film ("I'll probably bring my family," she says, "but it all seems so far away"), what it might be like to meet fans at conventions, or what sorts of interviews she might be invited to do in the future. "I thought people wouldn't even notice me," she says, "but everyone keeps telling me that even the small characters still get attention. I suppose if I keep getting interviewed, I'd better come up with better things to say!"

Zam Wesell has the coolest accessories and outfit since Boba Fett. Photo by Sue Adler.

ZAM WESELL

"I'd love to do more film, maybe even the lead. You can't really generalise a role, but I'd like to take on roles that are high energy, sexy, exciting, fun-loving characters. I love Audrey Hepburn's roles, for example.'"

- Leeana Walsman
bounty hunter Zam Wesell

Leeanna and costar Nathan Page in the production of *La Dispute* at the Sydney Theatre Company. Photos by Tracey Schramm.

[BELOW] Leeanna enjoyed her part as a fun-loving character in *Love is a Four-Letter Word*. Photo courtesy of ABC TV Photography

does not end happily. "It was terrible," she admits. "It all gets out of control. We were all like animals. The prince and princess end up stopping the experiment. The play's an open-ended thing, and the director is quite dark. So, we all got shot."

TRIP TO BOUNTIFUL

Her first day on the set, bounty hunter Zam Wesell came face-to-face with Obi-Wan Kenobi.

"I couldn't believe I was working with Ewan McGregor," Walsman says. "I was so excited to meet him, and I was so nervous! I didn't even know what accent to use on screen. In fact, I don't even know now what accent I ended up using! I didn't know if I was doing things right - honestly, the first line on the first day is the scariest moment in any production, and this was a big production."

On a set surrounded by blue screen, Walsman found out just how physical her role was to be as she worked with Obi-Wan and Anakin Skywalker (Hayden Christensen). The scenes were demanding, but Walsman was pleased with the level of action in her part. Getting into character, however, was a little more challenging.

"It's all about the costume," she says, noting that getting fixed up with outfits and weaponry took up plenty of time. In fact, various parts of her leather-and-Lycra costume, like the armour, had different crewmembers attending them, as did her guns. "I wear a helmet, but I have my own face most of the time. I briefly wear a veil so I can be anonymous, but it flies off at some point. That costume and the weaponry really help make the character. You look at yourself in the mirror, and you say, 'This is how I'm going to be.' And then it's all about dodging lightsabers, flying spacecraft, running down streets. It was all completely different than anything else I'd ever done."

Despite her grueling schedule at the time - she often needed to be on the set at 5 am for costume fittings, and in the evenings she continued to per-

> *"The costume and weaponry really help make the character. You look at yourself in the mirror, and you say, 'This is how I'm going to be.'"*
>
> *- Leeana Walsman*

form on stage in *La Dispute* - Walsman feels the 10 days she spent working on *Star Wars* were some of the best of her career thus far. "The set was so relaxed. I felt really happy and had so much fun. It seemed like a whole lot of people just doing amazing work. The spacecraft, the outfits, the weaponry – it's all astonishing. It was a calm, wonderful set to be on."

She attributes much of that comfortable working atmosphere to the demeanor of George Lucas himself. "He was very laid back," she remembers. "He never seemed to lose it. Some people can get so stressed in this business, but he was so in control all the time."

Still, she concedes that reading only her own scenes and part (instead of the entire script) and therefore acting "in the moment" was a little unnerving and disconcerting. "In some scenes, I don't even know where I am," she admits. "It'll all be put together later on. And only being there for

Zam Wesell takes aim in *Attack of the Clones*. Photo by Sue Adler.

ZAM WESELL

Zam's headgear features a set of specially equipped binoculars that enable her to hone in on her prey. Photo by Sue Adler.

10 days, it's scary to not know exactly where you are in the bigger scheme of things. I don't even know what it's going to look like in the end!"

Even after her scenes, a couple of chases, and a few of lines of dialogue were over, Walsman still found herself affected by her experience. "That something so big was so relaxed really affected me," she says. "I run into people now, and they say, 'Hey, I worked on your spaceship!' The Australian acting community is so small that we all know each other or know of each other. It's great. [There were] some very big stars are in this film, yet there was no 'star behaviour' from anyone. Everyone was patient and pleasant and great to work with. They were wonderful."

In the end, however, there are some drawbacks to being a bounty hunter and not a Jedi in the *Star Wars* galaxy.

"I didn't get to play with a lightsaber," Walsman admits. "But I'll tell you: I had a great gun. I was very pleased with my weaponry."

SETTING HER SIGHTS ON THE FUTURE

Along with millions of others, Walsman now waits for *Attack of the Clones* to hit the big screen. Between now and then, she'll visit California, and she'll brace herself for the reaction of fans worldwide - Walsman wonders whether Zam Wesell will have even a fraction of the popularity of the infamous Darth Maul or Boba Fett.

"I had no idea how big it was at the time," she says. "Honestly, I didn't even know what a bounty hunter was when they offered me the role. But I didn't want to admit that and look stupid, of course. So now I can't believe that I already have people sending me fan mail. I think that's surreal! Then there are these Internet sites where people are already talking about me and about my character. I think it's phenomenal. I hope everyone likes me."

She'll continue to act on stage in *Old Masters* until December. After that, she has her eye on Hollywood. "I think *Old Masters* is going to be the most difficult role I've done to date," she says.

"Some of the best actors in Australia are in this. I'm the youngest person on the stage, and I'm so excited to be working with them. But I'd love to work in Hollywood. I went to the States shortly after finishing *Star Wars*, and I got myself an agent and a manager over there. There are so many scripts to read – it's amazing! It focuses you. If you want to be an actress, you have to be everywhere, not just in Australia. You realise how much of a business it is when you visit Hollywood. They send me scripts, and I audition sometimes by sending a video back to the States. Still, it's much nicer to be there and do it face to face."

If her career advances as she hopes it will, Leeanna Walsman could be working on another film, possibly a Hollywood production, by the time Episode II opens in the summer of 2002. Given the fan reaction to previous bounty hunters from the saga, she could easily find herself in the spotlight as her name and face become known to millions of *Star Wars* fans all over the world. For now, Leeanna won't let herself get too excited about that possibility. "I still don't think it's ever going to happen," she says. "But who knows what'll happen? Ask me again in a year!" ☺

MY STAR WARS

JAIME KING'S VOCAL PERFORMANCE AS AURRA SING IN *STAR WARS: THE CLONE WARS* HAS GIVEN LIFE TO THE ENIGMATIC BOUNTY HUNTER. A POPULAR FIGURE AT CONVENTIONS, SHE'S ALSO A LIFELONG FAN OF THE SAGA! INTERVIEW BY MARK NEWBOLD AND JAMES BURNS

When did you first become aware of *Star Wars*?
When I was a toddler, it was my mother's favorite movie. She saw it multiple times in theaters when it came out.

What was your reaction to seeing *Star Wars* for the first time?
It was such a fantastic, unlimited universe that took me multiple viewings before I could understand the scope of the film.

Can you reveal something about yourself that will surprise *Star Wars* fans?
A producer wanted me to put cinnamon rolls on my ears and pretend to be Princess Leia in *Fanboys*, but of course I said no.

Do you have a favorite *Star Wars* scene?
The "I am your father" moment from *The Empire Strikes Back* is such an iconic scene for me. It contains one of cinema's most dramatic twists, and really highlights, through Vader, the dangers of having so much power that it can dominate your destiny. It ends with Luke literally taking a leap of faith and following his heart, which is a powerful message for everyone.

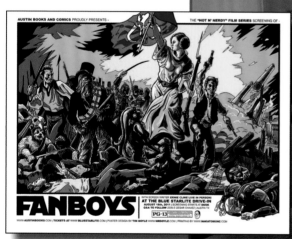

Where did you sign your first *Star Wars* autograph?
It wasn't until San Diego Comic-Con in 2009 after the first episode of *Star Wars: The Clone Wars* featuring Aurra Sing. I've been to a few more since then! I love the *Star Wars* fan community: They're the most fun and loyal fans one could ask for.

Bathroom image: Shutterstock
Fanboys poster by Tim Doyle
"Luke's Destiny" by Frank Stockton
Jaime King photo: Albert L. Ortega,
Contributing Photographer
Picture Group

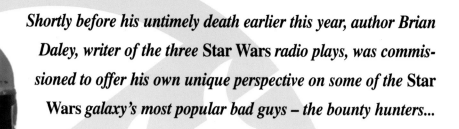

Shortly before his untimely death earlier this year, author Brian Daley, writer of the three Star Wars radio plays, was commissioned to offer his own unique perspective on some of the Star Wars galaxy's most popular bad guys – the bounty hunters...

THEY'RE THE GRIMMEST REAPERS.

They're beings who stalk the twilight free-fire zone between the law of the jungle and the retribution of governments. They're red of fang and claw, answerable to no one. Ruthless – respecting authority only when it's backed by naked force. Many are as criminal as their quarry. Their license to kill comes from the mint and their own dark drives. A name on a wanted notice empowers them to seek our prey, run it to the ground... capture or slay it.

Of all the frequently cited parallels between George Lucas' universe and the American Wild West, none is more dramatic or ominous than that of the bounty hunters. Sound like a career opportunity you'd like to know more about? Fine. Let's talk about job specs and other factors you'll want to consider. But first, a look at your competitors.

PREDATORS OF THE EMPIRE

A good many *Star Wars* viewers sensed that the bounty hunters were lurking nearby as soon as that festering nest of lethal rascality, Mos Eisley, came into view in *Star Wars IV: A New Hope.* How could it be otherwise, with manhunts, gunfights, stoolies and desperadoes figuring so prominently in the plot?

Late, unlamented Greedo had a technical claim to being the first bounty hunter to make an appearance in the mythos. Yet, despite his Rodian heritage, he seemed more of a petty gangster trying to make his bones. It wasn't until the rogue's gallery line-up on the bridge of Vader's Destroyer, *The Executor,* in *Star Wars V: The Empire Strikes Back,* that we got to see the real item and hear Admiral Piett's comment: "Bounty hunters! We don't need that scum."

Piett was whistling past the graveyard; the Empire likely couldn't get along without its independent contractors. The subject came up in a conversation I had with Jon Knoles, an animator for LucasArts Entertainment, Lucas' gaming division, whose work includes X-Wing, Dark Forces and the upcoming Shadows of the Empire. Jon points out the fact that the Emperor wasn't all powerful, despite his dark side mental powers and the ability to shoot electrical energy bolts from his fingertips. Thus he had Mara Jade, Vader and other lieutenants to run errands, oversee details and troubleshoot.

In the same way, Darth Vader didn't hesitate to do some out-sourcing of his own. Then, too, mustering the blood-

hounds on the bridge was likely the Dark Lord's way of letting it be known he wasn't happy with the lack of results from his starfleet assets. That served as a strong incentive to the military types; when Vader wasn't happy, underlings were liable to suffer the kind of choking episode no amount of Heimlich Manoeuvre could relieve.

As was the case in stories of the American frontier, the *Star Wars* bounty hunters have taken on an interest and a stature out of all proportion to their numbers. Who are they, and how do they come to be working their deadly trade? How do they fit into the greater scheme of things, and what will be their place in the upcoming *Star Wars* projects?

George Lucas' bounty hunters were based, of course, on similar characters in our own history. Yet, even there, facts and imagination have intertwined.

The popular image of the Western bounty hunter is of the freelance, for-profit outlaw trader tracker: Clint Eastwood's 'Man with no Name' in a *Fistful of Dollars* and its two 'spaghetti western' sequels, or Steve McQueen as Josh Randall in the sixties television series *Wanted, Dead or Alive.* But the real life practitioners of the trade mostly brought in wild animal pelts or Native Americans' scalps. (At that, authorities weren't very particular about the age, gender or even the tribe of the human victims.)

There were unquestionably those professionals who hunted wanted men – and women – for the rewards on their heads. But experts on the frontier say that our concept of the job is more a product of the 20th Century than the 19th.

For that matter, bounty hunters may well be more numerous today than ever. Bail-jumpers are the source of revenue. The 'skip-tracers' who hunt them down are integral to our criminal justice system.

It's not skip-tracers we're talking about in *Star Wars,* however, nor repo men nor summons servers. Boba Fett, Dengar, IG-88 and their ilk are cold-blooded predators, with no apologies.

Surely the Empire had greater need of them than it did the Old Republic. That was an age of comparative order. Evildoers had pursuers more fearsome than the most savage bounty hunter: the Jedi Knights.

The Empire, however, devoted most of its efforts to suppressing rebellion and shoring up its own power. Criminal justice took a back seat, and Imperials had scant time for seeking mere felons.

In fact, one of George Lucas' original concepts for *A New Hope* involved automated executioners. The spherical Jedi training remote on which Luke practices his lightsaber moves

A good many Star Wars *viewers sensed that the bounty hunters were lurking nearby as soon as that festering nest of lethal rascality, Mos Eisley, came into view in* A New Hope. *How could it be otherwise, with manhunts, gunfights, stoolies and desperadoes figuring so prominently in the plot?*

aboard the *Millennium Falcon* was the prototype of innumerable such airborne weapons. The concept was that they would wander population centres scanning for targets identifiable via their memory banks, terminating them on the spot.

The remotes weren't used that way, but something else filled the bill. Where local jurisdictions' authority ceased and the Emperor's minions were elsewhere engaged, the bounty hunters prospered.

In terms of bang for the buck, the mere announcement of a bounty would be almost as useful to the Empire as the bounty itself. At no cost beyond that of putting out the word, the Imperials enlisted billions of potential informers – a living sensor network that at the very least hampered the wanted individual's freedom of movement. No matter where the fugitive fled, someone (like Grea the Orfite from the West End Game's *Star Wars* Role Playing Game Elrood Sector book) would be on the lookout for them.

So why not an *Empire's Most Wanted* weekly television series?

There surely were criminal justice and military intelligence data networks, as well as public information systems. And word gets around the underworld faster than any starship. But the sheer size of a galactic government means there's too much information for any individual hunter or fugitive-spotting citizen to absorb. You could watch 500 channels of wants-and-warrants around the clock every day (if that was how your sensorium happened to be wired) and still not catch more than a fraction of all the bounty postings.

Then, too, you can't make a living by waiting for prime quarry to simply wander by. The pros have their own grapevines and data systems. Those winnow out the small-time mopes who aren't worth the trouble and the perps known to have gone to ground in far-off regions. That leaves a much more manageable roster of viable targets.

So, considering all this information, let's assume you've decided to seek your fortune in the exciting occupational speciality of bounty hunting. What career considerations should you be mulling?

First and foremost, there's the background skills you'll need to ensure that you're the pursuer and not the quarry. (Given the chequered past of the hunters we know about, it's probably not uncommon for bounty chasers to be gunning for each other.)

Individuals drawn to the trade are as varied as to origin as they are dangerous. Zuckuss the Gand, for instance, had been

Above: Princess Leia disguised as bounty hunter Boushh in Return of the Jedi

Left: Phlutdroid IG-88, one of the assembled "scum" from The Empire Strikes Back

Above: *Han Solo attempts to negotiate an overdraft from Greedo in* Star Wars

a 'findsman', hunting runaway slaves on his misty home-world. Dengar was a former swoop rider and gladiator. IG-88 started out as an assassin droid.

Previous experience in law enforcement or the military would be a major plus for you. So would proficiency as a big-game hunter, surveillance expert or bodyguard. If you come from a culture with a strong warrior tradition or a species that devotes much time to predation and combat, so much the better. Lacking those advantages, you should consider apprenticing yourself to a successful bounty collector.

Chose carefully, though. Many a long-lived veteran has survived by letting naive assistants take the risks. You can learn a lot by being shoved into a darkened room full of trigger-happy psychopaths, but the knowledge isn't likely to do you much good.

There are a number of schools, both above-board and covert, where you can acquire the necessary basic know-how – but there again wisdom counsels discretion. If you receive a useless diploma in hyperdrive repair, you're merely out of some money; if you get inferior training as an outlaw-tracker, it will put a severe crimp on your life expectancy.

Beyond your basic talents and proficiencies, you'll need to consider the question: Am I adaptable? Your prey may come from any of a huge number of species, and what works against one could spell disaster against another.

Your electrified smart-harpoon worked fine against that Squid Head pirate, but it's hardly a weapon of choice for going up against a Chiggnash extortion ring. After all, the Control Mind of the scorpion-like Chiggnash breeds warrior drones the way a termite queen lays eggs. That harpoon will short-circuit before you work your way through the first few dozen, and a conventional blaster won't do much better. Pop quiz: Then what do you do?

Similarly, it's one thing to go up against a screaming, slavering foe whose style is to charge head-on. But if you're after one that can blend in with its surroundings like a chameleon and pass for a patch of wall stucco, you'd better have sharpened your senses of hearing and smell.

You may also want to think twice before trying to cash in on a contract put out by the Hutts or similar underworld figures. The line from *Prizzi's Honour*, "They'd rather eat their children than part with money," applies quite literally to some of these folk. They might well decide to add you to the menu, thus economising on your payoff.

Whatever your *modus operandus* and weaponry, do not buy into the snake oil you'll hear about honour among bounty hunters. So-called rules of engagement, prerogatives of the first sighting... they're all smoke screen and hype. As events in *Shadows of the Empire* will prove, bounty hunters won't hesitate to attack their own, betray allies or whack a former companion.

No overview of this cruel breed would be complete without a more detailed mention of Boba Fett, the most successful, capable and charismatic bounty hunter alive (at

Right: *Boba Fett looks on as his prize, Han Solo, is frozen in* The Empire Strikes Back

Right: Darth Vader enlists some extra help in the search for the Millennium Falcon

least, as of this writing). Bits of the puzzle that is Fett have appeared over the years.

We know of his origins as Journeyman Protector Jaster Mareel, who's been described by several sources as 'ugly'. There are credible reports of his disgrace and dishonourable discharge from his law enforcement agency. How he got his new alias or acquired the rare Mandalorian battle armour he wears are secrets no one has yet penetrated with any degree of certainty.

To be sure, no other individual in his dire trade cuts as striking a figure as Fett. First and foremost there's that Mandalorian helmet. Its blacked-out, T-shaped visor slit, reminiscent of the Greek helms of Corinth and Boetia, gives him the look of both machine-like soldier and merciless executioner. The sight of it alone is enough to unnerve many opponents.

The rest of Fett's suit is just as impressive, making him a walking arsenal. His wide range of weapon options and a host of sensory and battle-management systems give him the capabilities of an entire hunter-killer squad.

Last but not least, there is his backpack jet pack. That feature has most of the advantages of a small personal transport vehicle and almost none of the drawbacks. Its mobility gives him a tremendous edge and adds to the romantic figure Fett cuts in the eyes of some. It provides him with the nearest thing most humans can know to the airborne freedom of birds.

Many rivals would avail themselves of such a jet pack if they could, but such systems are both difficult to procure and tricky to master. They require the combined virtues of an ace fighter pilot, master technician and interstellar-class athlete.

Fett has purposely left his attire battle-scarred and showing its long, hard use. To heighten the intimidation factor, he wears a clutch of Wookiee scalps at his right shoulder. They are proof that he has overcome some of the galaxy's best fighters and hunters, and that he's not a man who relents on a vendetta.

As to spacecraft, Fett has always, shrewdly, been at pains to provide himself with the maximum speed and firepower. While *Slave I* and its little used back-up, *Slave II*, were very different vessels, both fit the bill for pursuit (or escape), as well as combat.

In short, Boba Fett comes equipped with all the prerequisites of the bounty hunter: training, experience, motivation, equipment, versatility and a moral code that makes virtues of his flaws. He has scored startling triumphs and survived devastating defeats. It seems certain that the Force has spared him to play out some defining role in the great pattern of the *Star Wars* epic.

There remains the question of how the institution of boun-

ty hunting will fare as galactic history moves forward. The hunters' frequent patron, the Empire, is only a shadow of its former self. The re-emergent Republican government shows less enthusiasm for the profit-motive killers. More to the point, new Jedi have begun to take up the lightsaber in the service of galactic law and justice; each one greatly reduces the need for slayers-for-pay.

Yet, just as the Empire had its higher priorities, the Jedi and other forces of law and order will be kept busy guarding the fragile new freedom and stability. Competing, balkanised local governments have their own agendas and ethics. The underworld will still put out contracts on those it wishes to see eliminated. Will the bounty hunters fade away? The answer is a resounding no.

In anything short of a Utopia, there'll always be those who want others brought to accounts or eliminated. Lacking the wherewithal to do it themselves, they'll hire others to get it done. Inevitably, there'll be those ready, willing and able to oblige.

So long as money moves from hand to hand (to tentacle); so long as some have and others covet; so long as group hates group and an eye is demanded for an eyestalk... the grimmest reapers will have a cash crop to harvest. ■

Below: Darth Vader briefs bounty hunter Dengar in The Empire Strikes Back

McQUARRIE'S BOUNTY HUNTER VISIONS

Anyone familiar with the background of the *Star Wars* universe and its imagery knows the work of artist Ralph McQuarrie.

From the outset, Ralph's sketches and paintings have provided guiding visions and blueprints for the Lucasfilm cosmos. His experience at Boeing, Kaiser Industries and CBS News – particularly his work depicting *Apollo* space missions – made him a natural to give form, colour and texture to George Lucas' vision.

Asked about his contribution to the bestiary of the bounty hunters, Ralph recalls a time at Elstree Studios in England, during the filming of *The Empire Strikes Back*. While Lucasfilm was in the midst of building sets and so forth, *Empire* director Irvin Kershner rushed in, needing conceptual art. Someone mentioned the idea of bounty hunters.

Ralph made a few quick sketches that were whisked away to the prop crew. The guys there got to work, and three or four days later the rogues' line-up was on the soundstage. "(They just) turned up in the film... voila," the artist remembers.

Exact details are difficult to nail down after the passage of so much time. A sketch Ralph remembers as being the work of Costume Designer John Mollo most likely provided the basis of Zuckuss.

While the artists were working on the snowtrooper designs for the Battle of Hoth, Ralph did a helmet drawing that was adapted to the Boba Fett costume – which was, he says, essentially the creation of Visual Effects Art Director Joe Johnston. ■

PREDATORS FOR HIRE

A GUIDE TO STAR WARS BOUNTY HUNTERS

The Galaxy is full of law-abiding citizens happy to follow the directions of their planetary governments, as well as The Old Republic, the Empire or The New Republic. But the criminals among them are sometimes too much for the local law enforcement to handle. And with travel through space so easily accomplished, jurisdictions become a joke. Although common in the days of the Old Republic, bounty hunting became very popular under Emperor Palpatine's 'New Order'. Many hunters grew rich off the Empire's slave trade or rebel bounties, and bounty hunting guilds constantly sprang up. Some hunters became legends, while others became objects of the hunt themselves. Hunter and Hunted, Stalker and Prey... the Galaxy is a cold place when there's a bounty on your head.

BOBA FETT

Many legends and stories have arisen over the years about Boba Fett, the deadliest and most mysterious bounty hunter in the galaxy. He was once a moral journeyman protector named Jaster Mereel, but was exiled from the world of Concord Down after he killed a corrupt protector. Since the Clone Wars, Fett has worked as a mercenary, a soldier, a personal guard, an assassin and, most frequently, as the highest paid bounty hunter in the known systems. Clad in the fearsome armour of the Mandalorian supercommandos, Fett has modified it to become a walking arsenal. Aided by his well-equipped starship, *Slave I*, Fett is relentless as he tracks his prey. Fett has worked for numerous gang lords, including Jabba the Hutt, and for Imperials. When Darth Vader hired him to find Han Solo, a man who has mysterious links to Fett's past, the hunter was successful. Solo's friends later rescued him, causing Fett to rocket into the mouth of the Sarlacc at the pit of Carkoon on Tatooine. Boba Fett somehow survived, and is currently at large in the galaxy.

BOUSHH

During Emperor Palpatine's reign, the largest criminal organisation in the galaxy was Black Sun. One of the bounty hunters it employed was a slight Ubese named Boushh. Unfortunately for Boussh, he tried to get more credits for a hunt than he had agreed to, and Black Sun no longer had need of his services. After his disposal, the mane and outfit of Boushh was taken by Princess Leia, who eventually disguised herself as Boushh when she attempted to infiltrate Jabba the Hutt's palace. The plan almost worked, but Boushh was unmasked and Leia was put in jeopardy.

IG-88

Designed for a certain amount of autonomy and intelligence, the assassin droids of the Old Republic had been a law enforcement tool until misuse and reprogramming made them dangerous. When five IG-class droids were given semi-sentient programming at the high-security Holowas Laboratories, they escaped and slaughtered their creators. One droid, IG-72, became a bounty hunter in the Outer Rim Territories, while a second, IG-88, became one of the most fearsome bounty hunters in the Galactic Core. It joined in the Imperial search for Han Solo, even going so far as to ambush Boba Fett upon his return to Tatooine. Although IG-88 was apparently destroyed, it has since appeared in other parts of the galaxy. Meanwhile, the fate of the other three IG droids remains unknown.

ZUCKUSS

On the gaseous planet Gand, the tradition of bounty hunting is a revered art form. Gand 'findsmen' are highly superstitious, using ancient rituals and omens to divine the location of their quarry. Zuckuss was descended from a long and illustrious line of findsmen, but with the rise of the Empire he took to the skies. He became a tireless tracker whose affinity for intuiting his quarry's moves was due less to rituals and more, perhaps, to a latent manifestation of Force powers. Although he was a successful bounty hunter on his own, he was hired by Jabba the Hutt and paired with a brilliant rogue protocol droid named 4-LOM. The two worked well together, and after the death of Jabba, Zuckuss and 4-LOM roamed the galaxy together as a team in search of prey.

VALANCE

Once a gunner for the Empire, Captain Valance's promising career was ended when a Rebel attack torpedoed his emplacement. Left on the Telos-4 medical station to die, Valance was instead given the cyborg implants and survived. No longer able to fight for the Empire, the bitter man became a bounty hunter, leading a cadre of disenfranchised pirates and smugglers. After the destruction of the first Death Star, Valance attempted to track down Luke Skywalker and his rebel friends, but subsequently gained respect for the young Jedi-to-be. Later, while protecting a rebel, Valance was killed in a duel with Darth Vader.

GALLANDRO

Orphaned as a child by the revolutionaries and terrorists from Goelitz, Gallandro joined his planetary militia as soon as he was able. He was an exemplary soldier, but his lack of conscience and ruthlessness bothered his superiors. He became a mercenary and bounty hunter, his exploits gaining him the death mark on over a hundred worlds. Gallendro was quick on the draw with his archaic collection of blasters and pistols, and was eventually hired by the Corporate Sector Authority. Although he was adept with weapons, Gallandro almost met his match in a young Corellian pilot named Han Solo. After Solo tricked him, Gallandro tracked him down on a Xim treasure ship. Gallandro was faster than the smuggler, but he was killed by the lasers of a no-weapon security system.

DENGAR

If anyone in the galaxy hates Han Solo more than Dengar, it would be news to both of them. Dengar had once been a successful young swoop jockey on the professional racing circuit. When he accepted the challenge of an illegal race against a cocky young Corellian named Han Solo, Dengar crashed his swoop and sustained massive cranial trauma. He was kicked out of professional racing, and a bitter Dengar turned his burning hatred towards Solo. After a stint as a gladiator, Dengar became an assassin for the Empire, but his instability bothered his superiors. He later became a bounty hunter, and was hired by Darth Vader to find Solo. He failed, but crossed paths with the Corellian years later. Having helped Boba Fett heal after Fett's bout with the Sarlacc on Tatooine, Dengar teamed up with the mysterious hunter several times. Dengar vows one day to destroy Solo.

GREEDO

Poor Greedo wanted to be a bounty hunter in the worst way, and at that, he succeeded. A Rodian, Greedo grew up in a culture that prizes bounty hunters. His family fled to Rodia when he was young, escaping slaughter to relocate in the Corellian sector. On the spaceport moon of Nar Shaddaa, Greedo learned about the joys of bounty hunting from some disreputable hunters, and was unwittingly responsible for his family's death at the hands of the Empire. Greedo fled to Tatooine, where he was employed by Jabba the Hutt to find Han Solo. The overconfident young hunter cornered Solo in Chalmun's cantina, yet lost his life to the smarter, quicker pilot.

SKORR

Enhanced with cybernetic implants and aided by a small Rybet known as Gribbet, the bounty hunter Skorr was a common sight on Ord Mantell. When Han Solo and his Rebel friends landed

in the spaceport to repair the *Millennium Falcon,* Skorr tried to capture the Corellian to deliver him to Jabba the Hutt, using a captive Luke Skywalker and Leia Organa as bait. Han and Chewie rescued their friends and tricked Skorr into interfering with an Imperial Star Destroyer. Skorr was sent to the spice mines of Kessel, but he later escaped, teaming with a cadre of other hunters to capture Han Solo from the pirate Raskar. In a tussle with Solo, Skorr was killed when he accidentally shot himself with his own blaster.

BOSSK

The hatred between the reptilian Trandoshans and the hairy Wookiees is well documented. When the Empire enslaved Kashyyyk, the Wookiees' homeworld, many Trandoshans became bounty hunters, tracking down still-free or escaped Wookiees for their Imperial employers. One of the best of those hunters was Bossk, but despite his best efforts, he couldn't capture the underground Wookiee hero, Chewbacca. Once Bossk almost snared Chewbacca and his partner Han Solo, but the two tricked the reptilian, humiliated him and left him for dead. Bossk survived and later jumped at the chance to track the duo down for Darth Vader. Although he failed in that capture too, he still roams the galaxy in his light freighter, *Hound's Tooth,* hunting other prey.

JODO KAST

Crossing Boba Fett is not considered a smart move by most sentients in the galaxy, but Jodo Kast has been doing it for quite some time. Like Fett, Kast wears the armour of the Mandalorian supercommandos to aid him in his dangerous bounty hunts. However, Kast is not as well trained and has made some blunders in his career. Such mistakes might not matter, except Kast has allowed – and sometimes encouraged – people to think that *he* is Boba Fett, in order to drive up his bounty price. Kast has become more careful and meticulous in his planning of late. He prowls the Outer Rim Territories, trying to keep away from the real Fett and a potential confrontation. Kast knows that a confrontation will inevitably occur, but he plans to be the victor.

4-LOM

A protocol droid on the passenger line *Kuari Princess,* 4-LOM began engaging the ship's main computer in a series of games. As the games progressed, the computer and droid altered each others' programming, and 4-LOM consequently gained self-aware sentience. He eventually became a master thief and information broker to some of the galaxy's most powerful crime lords. Jabba the Hutt saw great potential in the droid and refitted him to allow violent actions, thus gaining the smartest bounty hunter in the galaxy. Jabba later teamed 4-LOM with the Gand findsman Zuckuss. They enjoyed mutual success, and continued to hunt as a pair for many years after Jabba's death. ∎

Text by Andy Mangels. Illustrations by Jason Palmer

ACTOR, WRITER, AND *STAR WARS* FAN SIMON PEGG FIRST CAME TO PROMINENCE IN THE BRITISH HIT SHOW *SPACED*. HE WENT ON TO PLAY A RELUCTANT ZOMBIE KILLER IN *SHAUN OF THE DEAD* AND SCOTTY IN THE *STAR TREK* REBOOT. HE VOICED BANDAGED BOUNTY HUNTER DENGAR IN *STAR WARS: THE CLONE WARS*. WORDS: BONNIE BURTON

When was the last time you saw a *Star Wars* movie and what were the circumstances?
Oddly enough, I watched *A New Hope* only a few weeks ago. I saw it on the shelf and had an urge to watch it. Like when you bump into an old friend and suddenly realize just how much you have missed them. It was like pulling on a familiar warm coat and made me feel very nostalgic and happy.

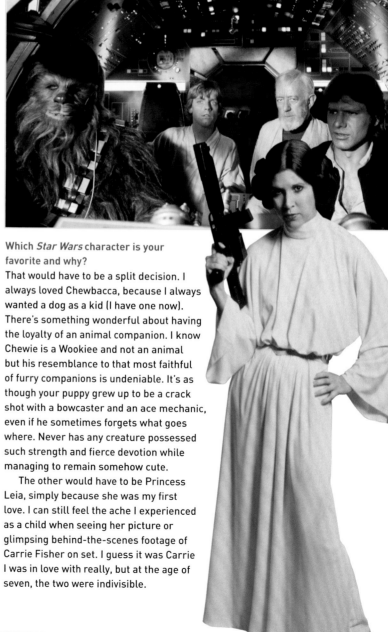

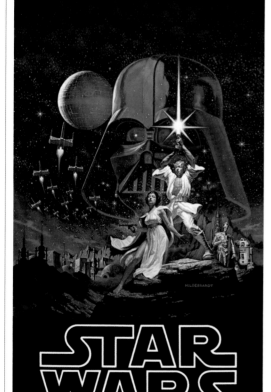

Which *Star Wars* character is your favorite and why?
That would have to be a split decision. I always loved Chewbacca, because I always wanted a dog as a kid (I have one now). There's something wonderful about having the loyalty of an animal companion. I know Chewie is a Wookiee and not an animal but his resemblance to that most faithful of furry companions is undeniable. It's as though your puppy grew up to be a crack shot with a bowcaster and an ace mechanic, even if he sometimes forgets what goes where. Never has any creature possessed such strength and fierce devotion while managing to remain somehow cute.

The other would have to be Princess Leia, simply because she was my first love. I can still feel the ache I experienced as a child when seeing her picture or glimpsing behind-the-scenes footage of Carrie Fisher on set. I guess it was Carrie I was in love with really, but at the age of seven, the two were indivisible.

Which *Star Wars* character is completely underrated and why?
Nien Nunb never gets the props he deserves. That flappy-faced Sullustan co-piloted the *Falcon* through the center of the second Death Star and helped take out its reactor core. Not only that, he was on his game 100 percent throughout that battle. He had his big black eyes on the Star Destroyers as well as the fighters and maintained a buffer of practical strategic defensive and offensive maneuvering, a perfect counter-point to Lando's recklessness. They were a formidable team and thanks to Nunb's careful pragmatic co-piloting, he helped save the Rebellion, and the entire galaxy.

What is your most prized *Star Wars* item?
I bought one of The Vader Project customized helmets at auction at *Star Wars Celebration Europe*. The helmet was customized by graffiti artists Dan & Dan and when I bought it, was yet to be finished. When they learned I had purchased it, they customized the design just for me. It's sky blue with an intricate pattern of characters and designs swirling around the faceplate and lower part of the helmet. On the left temple you can clearly see me and Nick Frost [Simon's friend and regular co-star] wearing bunny costumes. It's a prized possession.

EXPANDED

Be sure to catch Simon Pegg in the new movie *Paul*, as well as on Twitter at:
http://twitter.com/simonpegg

UNIVERSE

What is it about the original *Star Wars* films that make you want to watch them over and over again?
They had such an effect on me as a child. I owe them a debt of gratitude for expanding my imagination and cultivating my love for cinema, literature, and even music. They have huge emotional significance for me. I know the *Star Wars* galaxy is fraught with danger, but for me, it is a safe place to go if ever I feel out of sorts. It's a place I can escape to and feel happy.

Your movie *Paul* is about traveling around the U.S. with an alien. Who would you rather go on a road trip with: R2-D2 or Chewbacca?
Chewie! They'd both be good at keeping the vehicle going because they both have technical skills, but if we wanted to stop off and go for a hike, R2-D2 would be a bit of a drag, unless he used the little jet pack that none of us knew he had until 2002. Also I'd feel safer with Chewie going through some of the more remote areas. I've been into a few bars in Middle America; they can be like the Mos Eisley cantina. The music's good but you have to watch your step, particularly if you're from out of town.

ROGUES GALLERY

AN AUDIENCE

WHO'S WHO IN THE COURT OF THE GALAXY'S SLIMIEST CRIME LORD, BY LELAND Y. CHEE.

01: HERMI ODLE

02: KLAATU

03: MOSEP BINNEED

04: REVIDJASA

05: BOSSK

06: BOBA FETT

07: AMANAMAN

08: ORTUGG

09: NYSAD

10: SNIPP NKIK

11: HERAT

12: REE-YEES

13: YARNA D'AL' GARGAN

14: YOXGIT

15: RAYC RYJERD

16: J'QUILLE (TOOTH FACE)

WITH JABBA THE HUTT

17: GEEZUM

18: SAELT-MARAE (YAK FACE)

19: GAURON NAS TAL

20: ROGUA

21: TESSEK

22: JABBA DESILIJIC TIURE

23: BIB FORTUNA

24: TANUS SPIJEK

25: EPHANT MON

26: BUBO (BUBOICULLAAR)

27: A ROCK WART

28: DROOPY MCCOOL (SNIT)

29: SALACIOUS B. CRUMB

a fall of
SHAI

Eric Frederickson, previews the eagerly awaited Shadows of the Empire game for the new Nintendo 64, set for release in the UK and Europe early next year....

OWS

I don't know about the rest of you, but I already know what I'm asking for this Christmas. This coming December is slated to mark the release of Shadows of the Empire in the US, LucasArts' latest offering to the world of computer gaming. It will mark the culmination of a gargantuan multi-media campaign that has so far included a novel, a comic book series to be published as a graphic novel next year, a variety of toys from Hasbro, and a new trading card set painted by the Hildebrandt brothers. ▶▶

a fall of
SHADOWS

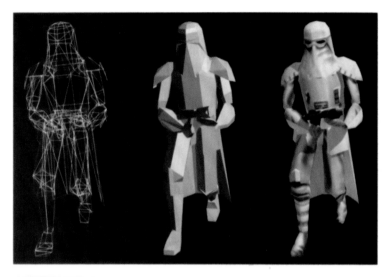

Left: *Imperial snowtroopers
– from wireframe roughs to
rendered virtual reality*
Below: *AT-AT attack
storyboards*

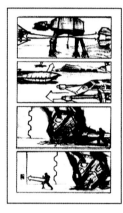
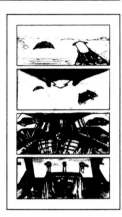

*Above: Boxing clever –
playtesting Shadows of
the Empire in secret*

Advance information on *Shadows of the Empire* has been scarce and hard to come by. For a long time there was something of a media blackout surrounding this new and exciting project. Those in the know knew what it was called, and how it fitted into the basic *Star Wars* continuity, but that was about all. This was due in large part to the fact that the Shadows video game was being developed parallel to and in co-operation with Nintendo's new Nintendo 64 video game platform. Nintendo was keeping a tight shroud of silence around their new top of the line system, and this lapped over onto the developers that were working with them.

Security on the project was akin to what one would expect working on the Manhattan Project. Bits and pieces of hardware, and specs on the Nintendo 64 machine, trickled in as they were developed. Designers working on the game were not allowed to discuss or share their work with their cohorts at LucasArts. When it came down to testing the game, members of the design team had to keep their hands in a box to keep passing co-workers from catching a glimpse of the Nintendo 64's revolutionary controller. As Jon Knoles, lead artist on the Shadows project put it, "We used to tell people that this controller was so unique that you stuck your hands in a box of ooze and it absorbed your thoughts."

If all the hype is to be believed, the final product will be well worth all this cloak and dagger nonsense. The Nintendo 64 was launched in Japan this April, and has so far been met with unparalleled success. By the first week of August, it had already sold over 900,000 units, and Nintendo predict that they will have shipped over five million units within their first nine months. Highlights of the system include anti-aliasing, Z-buffering, tri-linear mip map interpolation, and a load management feature... Now, before you go running in fear from all this high-minded techno-speak, give me a moment to explain what each of these will mean in terms of the ultimate gameplay experience!

Anti-aliasing and tri-linear mip map interpolation are just fancy ways of saying that the graphics look great. Anti-aliasing keeps polygon objects looking sharp no matter what angle you see them from. Tri-linear mip map interpolation keeps texture maps from looking blocky, even when extremely close up. The features combine to

COME TO THE DARK SIDE...

Below: The Outrider, *Dash Rendar's ship, in action*

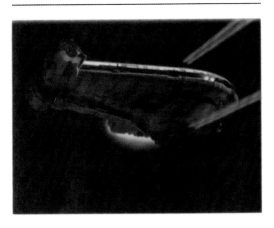

give you the cleanest, most realistic graphic objects you can expect to see anywhere.

The load management feature has a somewhat more direct effect on the way the game is played. On more primitive systems, distant objects will pop in and out of view, depending on how close to the viewer they happen to be. On the Nintendo 64, you will have no problems with buildings suddenly appearing as you race across Tatooine on your speeder bike. Objects appear on the horizon and gradually grow larger as you approach them.

Most impressive, however, is the Nintendo 64's Z-buffering feature, which allows for some of the best 3-D gaming you will ever see. Z-buffering, as Technical Lead Eric Johnston puts it, makes all objects in view "appear where they should in relationship to the rest of the environment from any perspective." Moreover, the Nintendo 64 uses a Reality Co-Processor that allows all this to be done in real time, without using software routines that eat up valuable CPU time. The Co-Processor handles a lot of the gruntwork of the graphics and sound, leaving the CPU free to work on giving the player the fastest, slickest gameplay possible. The practical upshot of this is that more complicated scenes and backgrounds will not slow the game down the way they would on lesser systems.

Wonderful as all these technical bells and whistles may be, they still, ultimately, only add up to pretty pictures and window dressing. Every video game is made or broken by its gameplay and, if we are to believe what we have been told, Shadows of the Empire promises to deliver in spades. Players will be run through a variety of different types of action, each with its own set of individual challenges, spread out over ten

In that same far away galaxy, where Luke Skywalker, Han Solo and Princess Leia battle the tyranny of the Empire, other characters and organisations also struggle for power, hidden in the shadows of the Imperial throne. Howard Roffman, the Vice President of Licensing at Lucasfilm Ltd, explains how this new story came together:

"We'd been doing extensions of the *Star Wars* universe in different types of media for several years, including the successful *Star Wars* novels," says Roffman. "Another significant medium was the Dark Horse comics. With those, we'd done a lot of spin-off stories based on *Star Wars*. And LucasArts was making new *Star Wars* stories in their games all the time.

"We thought it would be interesting to tie everything together and make it a real event. But the big question was, how do you go about making a story that is special enough to draw people in? To start with, we wanted to go back into the trilogy where familiar characters could be found and where you have the dramatic conflict between the Rebels and the Empire.

"After thinking about it, we decided that it would be very cool to explore this dark underworld of crime, which had been hinted at in the movies. There was already a suggestion that the underworld was in league with the Empire – when Darth Vader hires bounty hunters in *The Empire Strikes Back*, you can see the relationship is already there. We just expanded on this idea. We gave the crime organisation the name Black Sun, and we set up the leader of Black Sun in opposition to Darth Vader. On the one side of the Emperor you have Vader, on the other side you have the leader of Black Sun, and *Shadows of the Empire* is about this power struggle – at least in part."

In particular, *Shadows of the Empire* is the story of one heroic figure from the seedier side of the space lanes who helps the Rebellion behind the scenes. Although the novel and comic books will deal with many characters, the game will follow this hero's exploits as he dashes about the galaxy. The story begins on Hoth where our hero makes his initial Rebel connection with Han Solo. In fact, the character is a lot like Han – he's a smuggler and adventurer who inhabits the shadowy underworld of the Empire.

Later, the story continues between the times of *The Empire Strikes Back* and *Return of the Jedi*. "I always thought there were a

lot of unanswered questions about this time," Jon Knoles explained, "from Luke showing up in *Return of the Jedi* as a fully-fledged Jedi to Han being encased within Jabba's palace. How did that happen? Did Boba Fett just zip on over or did he run into some trouble along the way?"

"Jon is so immersed in the world of *Star Wars*," says Roffman. "He knows it and feels it and thinks it and breathes it, intuitively. Originally, Lucy [Wilson] and I were thinking that we would set it between *Star Wars* and *Empire*. Jon was the one who grounded us, saying that it's much richer to work between *Empire* and *Jedi*, because Luke now knows that Vader possibly is his father, and Vader is looking for Luke. There are all these other threads happening that create a rich dramatic content. And he was right. So the one sacrifice we had to make was that Han couldn't come out and play."

It was the absence of Han – frozen in carbonite – that partly led to the creation of the Han-ish character, Dash Rendar. "We definitely wanted to have a swashbuckler guy," Roffman remembers, "but there was also a story need for him. It was kind of inconceivable that Leia would embark on what she's doing, in terms of infiltrating (Xizor's organisation) Black Sun and trying to help Luke, without having somebody to watch over him. That's the basic role Dash plays in this, although it becomes a much more complicated role."

It was Roffman who presented the *Shadows* idea to George Lucas for his blessing. "He liked it a lot," says Roffman. "In his writing on *Star Wars*, he always looks to parallels in the real world. And he liked the idea of going off in this direction.

"George didn't add story input, in the sense of changing the contours of the story. The biggest advice or guidance he gave was to have it as grounded in reality as possible; the kind of things that happen in the story have to make sense, as if they would work in the real world.

"He's very conscious... of creating things that exist in a fantastic environment but not an illogical environment. If you have a story where you screw up your face and say, 'Hmm, some person wouldn't act like that,' then you've lost your audience. No matter how fantastic the special effects or technology is, you've created something that isn't plausible." ■

The Nintendo 64 game may be the centrepiece of the *Shadows of the Empire* property, but it won't be the only game in town. Steve Perry's novel has already been released ahead of the game by Transworld. The novel delves into the conflicts and motivations of new hero Dash Rendar and the other

characters, both new and old, who enter the story. The Dark Horse comic series, concentrating on the bounty hunters who have been hired by Jabba to hunt down Han Solo, will be compiled into a graphic novel by Boxtree, alongside their fascinating *The Secrets of Shadows of the Empire* guide by Mark Cotta Vaz. References to events in the novel will also be found in the comic books and in the game. The Nintendo 64 game represents the chance for fans to enter the world of *Shadows* and experi-

ence the thrills that they have read about in the novel and comics.

But Lucasfilm goes even further in providing unique *Shadows* experiences. They have created a soundtrack with theme music for characters and a symphonic score, which was written by Joel McNeely. The music will be used in the Bantam talking book edition of the novel, and card company Topps has commissioned some stunning new paintings based on *Shadows* from the Brothers Hildebrandt for a series of trading cards.

There will be a *Shadows of the Empire* collectible trading card expansion set for the *Star Wars* card game, too. ERTL also have two tie-in kits – the Emperor, released last month (reviewed elsewhere this issue) and Prince Xizor, due for release next year. Watch out also for Toy Options Shadows of the Empire Micro

Machines range, and Hasbro's terrific looking *Shadows*-inspired action figures. These include Dash Rendar, Luke Skywalker in Coruscant armour and a disguised Chewbacca.

The initial concept of treating a game like a movie property, with all the spin-offs and licenses that you would expect from a major Hollywood release, began at LucasArts. Once the writers, illustrators and game developers were at work, Roffman delved into another part of the original concept: bringing other key licensees into the *Shadows* mix.

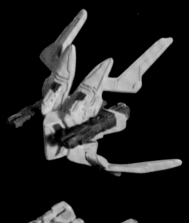

"We were walking a fine line," admits Roffman, "because we didn't want to make it a merchandising free-for-all. That's not the idea of *Shadows*. I see it much more as a platform for a lot of creative people to express their love of *Star Wars*, a better version of what we've been doing all these years with books, comics and games. As far as I'm concerned, if a product isn't contributing something new and creative, then it's not going to happen. You look at everything we've been doing all these years with books, comics and games. Look at everything we're doing, where we are making extensions, they're all areas that allow very gifted people to bring their own creativity to bear on the *Star Wars* universe."

After checking out all the video game systems, they turned to Nintendo and the Nintendo 64. In fact, the LucasArts developers were one of the first groups to see the early Nintendo 64 specs. As it turns out, it was a sweet deal for both companies, despite the delayed release of the game. Nintendo got a great license and game from LucasArts, while LucasArts got cutting-edge technology and a huge video game marketing machine from Nintendo. But in the end, of course, it will be the gamers who get the sweetest deal... ∎

a fall of
SHADOWS

Above: Another view of Dash Rendar's ship, the Outrider

locations, with many containing multiple stages.

The game opens up with a bang on the icy plains of Hoth, as the player takes on the role of roguish smuggler Dash Rendar, piloting a snowspeeder through one of the best flight simulations you will ever see. You experience full 360 degree freedom within a two mile circumference basin. The object of this level is to bob and weave through the legs of Imperial AT-AT walkers, and take them down with harpoon cables as Luke and his cohorts did in *The Empire Strikes Back*. In addition to the full 360 degree movement, you also get to choose camera views from inside the cockpit, from the rear of the snowspeeder, or from a variety of other perspectives.

Once time runs out on the snowspeeder sequence, the player moves on to Echo Base to take part in the escape sequence we all know from *Empire*. The action is first person, in the style of Dark Forces or Doom, though the play is apparently far superior, requiring more of the player than simply shooting at everything that moves inside a 2-D maze.

From this point, play moves off into space, where Dash, manning the gunnery controls of his ship, the *Outrider*, must make his way through an asteroid belt while fending off pursuing TIE fighters. Completion of this level takes you on to Stage II, and the search for the elusive bounty hunter, Boba Fett.

The search begins with a starship graveyard, and moves on to a seemingly abandoned weapons factory on the planet Peradon. The action once again is first person firefights, in which the player encounters, among other adversaries,

"The action stages aren't just 2-D mazes... For one thing, they were designed by the Dark Forces team and architectural students so it isn't just a jumble of mazes, but structures with logical functions for the Star Wars universe. We also wanted to make them truly 3-D, and that meant giving them a vertical component.

"This isn't like in a CD game where you have one pre-rendered path to follow. For example, you have freedom to move your speeder in the street [in Mos Eisley], or down side streets that might lead to a short cut."

Mark Haigh-Hutchinson, Project Leader and Senior Programmer

Left: Virago, *Xizor's ship*

"You have to be aware of things all around you and above you in Shadows. Strategically, there's a lot of area to explore. We've also hidden a lot of things here."

Jon Knoles, Shadows game lead artist

other bounty hunters such as Zuckuss, 4-LOM, and the infamous IG-88.

Information taken from IG-88 leads the search to the planet Gall, where the player starts off piloting the *Outrider* through a treacherous gorge. From there, it's into an Imperial base where Dash steals a jet pack and faces off against Boba Fett himself. Having distinguished himself by defeating the villainous bounty hunter, the player moves on to Stage III, wherein he is recruited by Princess Leia to shadow and look out for none other than Luke Skywalker.

This new bodyguarding assignment leads Dash, as one would expect, to Tatooine, and the Mos Eisley cantina. At the cantina, he overhears a biker gang setting out to do in Luke. This leads to an intense chase and fight scene on swoops, souped up speeder bikes. The action is similar in style to the 'Road Rash' racing game, and this sequence promises to be

Below and right: New interpretations of Mos Eisley created for Shadows of the Empire

one of the highlights of the game. The encounter with the swoop jockeys leads Dash to Luke, and an assault on a bulk freighter carrying plans for a new Imperial secret weapon (We'll give fans just one guess as to what that weapon is.). The player starts off piloting the *Outrider* on strafing runs against the freighter, after which he moves inside and on to another first person commando-style raid. Stage III ends with the revelation that Princess Leia has been captured by the notorious crime lord, Prince Xizor.

The chase leads to the Imperial planet Coruscant, where Dash personally infiltrates the evil Prince's fortress. As the thermal charges he has set go off, the player must pilot the *Outrider* through a series of access tunnels, in a sequence very much reminiscent of the *Millennium Falcon*'s flight through the Death Star in *Return of the Jedi*. This takes Dash to the climactic space battle with Xizor's armada and his skyhook base. If all goes well, Xizor's treachery is his downfall, and the Rebel Alliance once again wins the day.

While outstanding graphics and superior gameplay may provide the foundation upon which this game's success will be built, one should not downplay the strength of the story that the game is based on. It is this story, and the way it fits in with the greater *Star Wars* epic, that makes Shadows of the Empire a signature LucasArts project, and what will, in the long run, help set it apart from the video game pack.

Cinematic interludes spaced in between the various levels give the player a feeling of greater interactivity and control. By assuming the role of Dash Rendar, players get to make themselves part of the Rebel war effort, and take an active part in the greatest epic of our generation. Each one of us has, at some point or another, wanted to be out on the

THE HOME WAR!

For nearly 10 years, games developers have been trying to bring the definitive Star Wars experience into the home, and with Shadows of the Empire it looks like LucasArts has finally succeeded. But what of those that went before? Here's a brief guide to some earlier games...

Below: Boba Fett and Slave I, Nintendo 64 style

field of battle with Luke Skywalker or Han Solo. Once December rolls around, and Shadows of the Empire is released, we'll all get our chance.

The Shadows story also does more than give the players a vicarious thrill. It is more than a simple addendum to the great trilogy. Shadows has been smoothly woven into the epic's greater continuity, and serves to touch on and detail a number of themes and ideas that the three movies were unable to fully explore. The criminal underworld has always been a strong presence in the movies. Shadows covers in greater depth how this extensive underworld relates to and works with the dark Empire. The story gives us further insights into already familiar characters, such as Darth Vader and Boba Fett, as well as giving us new players to follow through this saga.

What all of this boils down to, in the final analysis, is a whole lot to get excited about. LucasArts and Nintendo are joining forces to bring us a new addition to our favourite story, one that's been licensed and approved by the grand storyteller himself, and one that's going to provide us each with a rather unique opportunity to interact with and be part of the greater story. It's going to be a couple of years before any of us gets even a peek at the other chapters of the epic. In the meantime, I'm going to take what I can get when I can get it, and I'm going to be thankful for it.■

With thanks to Dave Upchurch and all at Nintendo Magazine System. Distributor THE has announced that Shadows of the Empire will be released on 1 March in the UK and Europe. Predators of the Empire, Page 22.

Atari's *Star Wars* coin-op was a 3-D shoot'em-up that appeared in arcades back in the early eighties. Based on the film's climactic battle, it consisted of three stages: dogfighting TIE fighters in space, shooting gun towers on the Death Star's surface, and a final flight down the trench to the Death Star's exhaust port.

This was followed by The Empire Strikes Back, another 3-D shoot'em-up in a very similar vein. Here, however, you battled Imperial droids and giant AT-AT walkers on the surface of the ice planet Hoth, before heading into space to dodge tumbling asteroids as you evaded pursuing TIE fighters.

For the inevitable Return of the Jedi game, Atari dumped the wire frame 3-D in favour of a less-than-impressive isometric 3-D view, which took the player through the forest of Endor on a speeder bike and into the innards of the Death Star in the *Millennium Falcon*. All three Atari coin-ops were later converted for the home by Domark.

Star Wars fever finally reached the Nintendo Entertainment System in the form of an action-packed platform romp, in which you controlled Luke as he ventured from Tatooine to Yavin, battling stormtroopers along the way. For an 8-bit game it was graphically very impressive, although the gameplay was simplistic.

All three *Star Wars* movies have had the 16-bit Super NES treatment. Graphically exquisite, the games allow you to control your own choice of hero as you hop, skip and blast your way through level after level of platform action. Occasional 3-D-ish bits, like this walker battle from Empire, provided shoot-'em-up breaks.

One of the finest *Star Wars* games so far created is LucasArts' X-Wing, a marvellous (if slightly complex) spaceflight simulation in which you get the chance to pilot a choice of Rebel ships in a series of missions against the Empire. This was followed by TIE Fighter, which told the same story from the dark side.

Also from LucasArts came Rebel Assault, a CD-ROM game. It was essentially a gameplay-free (albeit good-looking) shoot'em-up, where the player ran through animated scenes shooting anything that moved. Rebel Assault 2, released last year, proved a slicker version of the game.

After X-Wing, the best *Star Wars* game around at the moment is Dark Forces, loosely described with affection as 'Doom with stormtroopers' but with a bit of puzzle-solv-

ing thrown into the mix. However, unlike Shadows of the Empire, the enemy soldiers are just scaled sprites, not proper 3-D objects. Barring any unforeseen movements in the Force, Dark Forces will be available for Sony Playstation in March next year, the first LucasArts game for that platform.

AND COMING UP... X-WING vs TIE FIGHTER MULTI-PLAYER SIMULATION
UK Release: November 1996
The first *Star Wars* network game offering a highly advanced space combat simulation for PC CD-ROM. The game can be configured in single player mode or multi-player, which will allow up to eight players to team up as a squadron or compete against each other via modem or a local area network.

JEDI KNIGHT: DARK FORCES II
US Release: early 1997
A 3-D, first-person, action adventure for Windows 95 which will enable players to battle the evil Empire with lightsabers and gain strength from using the Force. The game offers a multi-player option much demanded by *Dark Forces* fans.

REBELLION
US Release: first quarter of 1997
An epic real-time competition of galactic expansion and domination pitted against survival and resistance in the *Star Wars* universe. Players get to be strategic commanders of all resources, planets and forces controlled by the Galactic Empire or Rebel Alliance and are offered a universe of possible game scenarios.

LucasArts latest collection of four *Star Wars* games, LucasArts Archives Vol. II: The Star Wars Collection, is already on sale in the US. This features a collection of Rebel Assault, Rebel Assault II: The Hidden Empire, the TIE Fighter Collector's CD-ROM as well as Dark Forces Super Sampler Edition – plus the fascinating CD-ROM Making Magic: A Behind-the-Scenes Look at the Making of the *Star Wars Trilogy Special Edition*. This 'making of' CD-ROM includes an exclusive interview with George Lucas and a limited sneak preview of the digital enhancements from the *Star Wars Trilogy Special Edition*. As we went to press it was not known if the collection would be available in the UK. ■

CASTING

Shadows of the Empire stars many familiar characters from the Star Wars film trilogy, plus several new faces

PRINCESS LEIA & CHEWBACCA

Few individuals, male or female, could endure the hardships that Leia confronts in her travels as a leader of the Rebel Alliance. Her dedication to the cause is tested by her desire to save Han, but her inner strength enables her to overcome every obstacle – including the seductive powers of Xizor. When she suspects that Luke's life is again in danger, Leia is compelled to thwart the plot. In disguise and with the ever-faithful Chewbacca (also incognito) at her side, Leia delves into the mysterious and dangerous world of Black Sun, where she must summon up tremendous courage, even at the risk of her own life.

"We felt from the beginning of the story that we wanted to give a strong role to Leia," says Howard Roffman, "to put her in a position where she is very assertive, where she takes control of the situation and gets into a position of jeopardy because of it. The confrontation between Leia and Xizor, pretty much from the beginning, was an integral part of the story."

LUKE SKYWALKER

Following his cataclysmic fate at the end of *The Empire Strikes Back* – the lightsaber duel with Darth Vader in which Luke loses a hand and learns that Vader is his father – the fledgling Jedi Knight returns to Tatooine to regain his strength and resume his training. Yet he is drawn into several new adventures: an attempt to rescue Han Solo from Boba Fett; a space battle to intercept top-secret plans for a second Death Star; an attack by a marauding gang of swoop bikers; and a daring escape after being kidnapped by bounty hunters. Finally, Luke leads an assault on Xizor's palace, is reunited with Leia, and defeats the Dark Prince.

C-3PO & R2-D2

Threepio and Artoo have become fixtures in Luke's life ever since his uncle bought the droids from Jawa traders years ago on Tatooine. Their servitude and loyalty have endeared them to the Alliance, and their back-and-forth banter provides needed moments of levity. In *Shadows*, while Artoo assists Luke aboard his X-wing in a couple of pitched space battles, C-3PO teams with Leia in her scheme to infiltrate Black Sun. The droids are eventually together again aboard the *Falcon*, which they must manoeuvre – a sometimes hairy assignment – during the attack on Xizor's palace.

SHADOWS

Here's the **Shadows** *cast, with a synopsis of each character's pivotal role in this latest adventure.*

DASH RENDAR & LEEBO

He has the ego and swagger of a fellow smuggler – Han Solo – and Dash even does a good job, as Han did, keeping Luke out of harm's way. Driven by different motives, though, Dash joins the Rebels in resisting the Empire. At the helm of his starship, the *Outrider*, and accompanied by his sidekick droid, Leebo, he fends off TIE fighters and flies in the face of Xizor's mighty minions. In the end, Dash overcomes a perceived personal failure and joins the fray against Xizor on and above Coruscant.

LANDO CALRISSIAN

The life of a swashbuckler, as Lando would testify, has its highs and lows. He had it good as Baron Administrator of Cloud City, but after helping Luke and Leia escape from Darth Vader's clutches, he's now high on the Empire's enemies list. Lando relishes his life of danger and volunteers to assist the Princess, first in her attempt to retrieve Han and later in storming Xizor's fortress and the ensuing space battle over Coruscant. Despite earlier doubts, there's no mistaking in *Shadows* where Lando's allegiance lies.

BOBA FETT

The bravest, boldest, baddest and most mysterious bounty hunter in the galaxy has his hands full trying to deliver Han Solo to Jabba the Hutt. Solo, securely encased in carbonite aboard Fett's *Slave I* and with Jabba's hefty bounty on his head, is also coveted by two very different factions, both trying to intercept Boba Fett before he reaches Tatooine. Princess Leia, Solo's beloved, flies to Gall with Dash and Lando, but their retrieval attempt fails. Jealous bounty hunting brethren can't outwit Fett, either.

DARTH VADER

Beneath his powers of evil, drawn from the dark side of the Force to which he has succumbed, Vader still retains shades of his former 'good' self, Anakin Skywalker. After revealing to Luke Skywalker that he is his father, Vader pledges to the Emperor that the young Jedi, too, will be converted to the dark side – or die. Yet when confronted by that mission, and once he learns that Xizor has set out to kill Luke, Vader permits remnants of his paternal instincts to surface. While he hardly lightens up on his tyrannical ways, especially versus Xizor, the Dark Lord struggles with his moral duality.

CASTING SHADOWS

GURI

At first glance, she's a beautiful, intelligent and dedicated woman. Look deeper, and Guri is revealed as a lethal weapon in the service of Xizor. She's also a human replica droid for which her master had paid dearly. It is a wise investment. Guri is not only blindly loyal, but is programmed never to blink a synthetic eye when displaying her superior strength in disposing of Xizor's enemies. Even as her boss' world is about to crumble, she goes up against the best – Luke Skywalker – who spares her artificial life. But can she survive the explosion that blows Xizor's palace to smithereens?

JIX & BIG GIZZ

A popular sport throughout the galaxy is racing souped-up airspeeders called swoops. They are also the vehicle of choice among outlaw bikers known as swoop gangs, which are often hired by crime lords to smuggle spice, run weapons and carry out other illegal deeds. Big Gizz is a notorious biker whose gang works for Jabba. Darth Vader, well aware of the 'relationship', orders one of his unsavoury agents, Jix, to infiltrate Big Gizz's gang. The rationale is that once Boba Fett delivers Han to Jabba, Luke Skywalker – Vader's prime target – will surely follow. Jix's orders are to keep the Dark Lord apprised of activities at Jabba's palace.

XIZOR

His humanoid species, the Falleen, had evolved from reptiles. Xizor may not crawl on his belly like one, but he embodies other characteristics of a snake. Slithery leader of Black Sun – the most venomous crime organisation in the galaxy – Xizor is instinctually sly, cunning and clever. He grovels before the Emperor, yet knows that Palpatine's evil empire couldn't exist without his corrupt syndicate. The self–serving Dark Prince uses that influence in plotting to assassinate Luke Skywalker, a scheme that would exact revenge upon his dreaded rival, Darth Vader, and clear Xizor's path to his supreme goal: total control of the Empire.

Following advice from George Lucas that the *Shadows* story should be grounded in the real world, Roffman, Wilson and Knoles conceptualised Xizor. "We started thinking about the characteristics of this person. Even though the Godfather comes to mind, we didn't want to make him like Don Corleone, who is ultimately a fairly warm person, and also it would seem really corny and derivative. We felt it would be more interesting to go in a different direction, which was to make him colder, more calculating, a very accomplished being, somebody who had had a very difficult life but had risen out of it and was a perfectionist. He practices martial arts, enjoys the fine things of life, but also comes from a species that is basically reptilian – calculating, deceptive."

SHADOW WRITING

Dave Phillips talks to author Steve Perry about his best-selling novel,

the best known part of the **Shadows of the Empire** *saga to date...*

The writer of over 30 novels, 48-year-old Steve Perry is clearly delighted to now be part of the *Shadows of the Empire* multimedia event. For a man whose past credits include *Conan* and *Aliens* novels, television stories and his own imaginative creations, the opportunity to write a 'Godfather' style chapter of the *Star Wars* saga was just too good to pass up.

"Tom Dupree at Bantam and I had worked together before, on the novelisation of the film, *The Mask*," says Perry, explaining how he was first approached to write *Shadows of the Empire*. "Between that and my *Aliens* novelisations for them, he thought I might be able to play in the *Star Wars* universe, so he put me up to bat at Lucasfilm. They read some of my stuff and let me take a swing."

With *Shadows* proving such a high profile project, Perry and the rest of the team involved spent a lot of time preparing the ground to co-ordinate the different aspects, planned to offer different chapters of one overall multimedia story. "We all sat down ahead of time together – well, not all of us, but a bunch of us – and hammered out an outline that everybody could live with," Perry explains. "The outline was the basis for almost everything that followed. I think the Hildebrandt brothers used my book as inspiration for some of their illustrations [for the Topps trading card set], but Lucasfilm generated some visuals that everybody had to use."

I wondered how Perry found working in the established *Star Wars* universe compared to writing what came strictly from his own creations. "It's both easier and harder," he says. "Easier, because somebody has done all the background work, laid in a solid template you can use. And harder for the same reason – you're limited by somebody else's bounds; the language, which characters you can kill off, etc.

"That said, it saved me tons of research, and allowed me to answer questions I wanted to know the answers to, and I got to work with the gang at a time when they were young and full of fire and didn't have so much history. Plus I got to get inside Darth Vader's head, something nobody else has done in a long time. Even though everybody knows how it winds up, I still get a lot of "I couldn't put it down" comments. I love to hear those.

"There's some nervousness about being read by a whole bunch of people who really know the universe in which you are working. It's scary, you want to be sure to get it right. But I also knew going in, from talking to the other writers, that I wasn't going to please everybody.

Left: "It's scary," says Steve Perry, "you want to be sure to get it right."

"My favourite story about this concerns a note I saw posted on an AOL forum about the time I was wrapping up the outline. The note said, 'Bad news, folks, very bad news. Steve Perry is writing *Shadows of the Empire*.' Man, I'd been blasted before I even got the outline done! (Later, the writer of that note apologised and we get along fine, now.) But I knew I was going to get flak no matter what I wrote, so I just did the best I could and hoped most of the fans would approve. So far, the percentage seems to be about 9-to-1 in my favour."

Did he have much contact with the other *Star Wars* authors while writing the book?

"I talked to several of the other writers – Kevin J. Anderson, Timothy Zahn, Kris Rusch, Barbara Hambly, A.C. Crispin – and I exchanged a couple of notes with Michael Stackpole. Kevin sent me research material, as did Lucasfilm, and Bill Smith at West End Games. Mainly, the other writers and I traded some minor characters to avoid conflicts with other stories. For instance, Kevin's character

Above: The cover of the Bantam novel. "Xizor was a lot more handsome in my mind's eye than he turned out," says Perry

Durga the Hutt [who appears in *Darksaber*] has a small part in *Shadows*. I used one of Michael's pilots from *X-Wing Squadron*, too. Stuff like that."

One of the most impressive parts of the *Shadows* story is the new character, Xizor. I wondered who created the Falleen race, and Xizor in particular for the storyline.

"Lucasfilm gave me Xizor's name and occupation but I was allowed to fill him out, developing his ethnic background and species, general look, psychology and physiology," Perry reveals. "I also came up with the name for the organisation, Black Sun – which was intentionally based on the Japanese Yakuza and the Italian Mafia – and his lieutenant, Guri. Actually, I came up with pretty much all the characters we used, plus a bunch we didn't have room for. The meeting at Skywalker Ranch where we made outline notes was where we winnowed that list. I think it was Jon Knoles who named Dash's ship and designed it.

"People were throwing out ideas left and right and it was hard to keep track of who said what. I was afraid they wouldn't let us have two villains' viewpoints, but Tom Dupree fought to get Vader's viewpoint. I must admit, Xizor was a lot more handsome in my mind's eye than he turned out."

Moving on to the final book itself, the first two chapters of Perry's novel contain many passages regarding what many fans consider to be 'hallowed ground', i.e. scenes from the films. "The scenes in the book that came from the movie were as accurate as I could make them," Perry says. "I watched until I had every word and gesture, the colour and background, sounds and what I imagined it smelled like. It was as close to verbatim as I could get things, anyway. I got all kinds of help on this, mostly from Tom Dupree at Bantam; Howard Roffman, Lucy Wilson, Sue Rostoni and Allan Kausch at Lucasfilm, all of whom read what I did and offered useful and intelligent suggestions."

But was there something he had wanted to add to the *Star Wars* universe that he really liked that Lucasfilm asked to have removed from the final manuscript?

"There was one scene I tried to sneak into *Shadows*," Perry admits. "Lando and Luke need to contact Leia while they are in the *Falcon*. I had them find a ship refuelling dock, stop, and make the call to Chewy from there. I thought it was pretty clever how I slipped it in, but Bantam and Lucasfilm caught me. ('No, Steve, you can't have them pull into the gas station to use the phone, sorry.')"

With *Shadows* now a distant memory for Perry, he's busy on other projects. He's working on a novelisation of Leonard Nimoy's Tekno Comic book series *Primortals* for BIG Entertainment and Warner Books, and his latest novel, *The Trinity Vector*, was published by Ace in the US recently. "They're calling it 'A novel of technology and transcendence.' Me, I'd call it a near-future SF thriller, and rated X," laughs Perry. Beyond that he's also busy with a movie script based on the Dark Horse comic *Black Cross*, a collaboration with Chris Warner, but as yet has no further plans for any future *Star Wars* novels. "I'd be happy to work there again," he says, "But there's nothing on the docket as yet..."

Finally, I wondered if the author, busy though he is, would be getting a complimentary Nintendo 64 to play the game when it comes out? "I wish!" grins Perry. "I don't know how many of the toys and games and posters I'll get, but I hope they put me on the list to get them all. I love this stuff!" ∎

Shadows of the Empire is available in hardback now, published by Bantam. The book is also available in paperback.

Harrison Ford
on Playing Heroes, Handling the
Paparazzi,
and Returning as
Indiana Jones

By Gabriela Tschamer-Patao

HERO

W hen the American Film Institute recently announced its list of the best movie heroes of all times, Harrison Ford claimed two honors. He placed #14 as the cocky smuggler Han Solo in the *Star Wars* movies and took the #2 spot as the adventurous archeologist Indiana Jones. As cleverly written and carefully crafted as these roles are, the actor made a large contribution to their heroic appeal. His rugged good looks, dry wit, and everyman charm are perfect qualities for adventurers who discover hidden treasures, rescue damsels in distress, outwit the bad guys, and, incidentally, save the world.

In a career spanning more than 30 years, Ford has played presidents and police officers, doctors and secret agents. None of his roles, however, has made such a lasting impact on popular culture as Han Solo and Indiana Jones. Ford credits the movies themselves for the popularity of his characters. "They are as near as you come to classic films these days," he explains during a recent press session to promote *Hollywood Homicide* in Beverly Hills. "Each generation is introduced to them as they grow up, and the DVD release of the Indiana Jones trilogy will only add to that. It has helped my career enormously that young people know me through these films."

Some of Ford's recent films-notably Random Hearts (1999), K-19: The Widowmaker (2002), and Hollywood Homicide (2003)-have not been huge box-office hits. Sure, he'd like a big hit, says Hollywood Homicide director Ron Shelton. "We all need a hit. But Harrison is a smart actor who makes interesting choices. He'll work for a long time." However, with the release of the Indiana Jones DVD Set on October 21, and the prospect of a fourth installment of the series masterminded by George Lucas and Steven Spielberg in his future, the slight bump in Ford's career will soon be a thing of the past.

He explains the process of making an Indiana Jones movie as follows: "George develops the script with a writer, this time Frank Darabont. Then

Whether charming the ladies, punching out the bad guys, or punching up to lightspeed, Ford's characters bridge the gap between the every-man and the hero.

it goes to Steven, and he has a few weeks with the writer, and then he comes to me with the script. By that time it's supposed to be perfect." Ford pauses for a couple of seconds and adds with a laugh, "But it never is. We all agree on a concept and a general tone before we get started. Therefore, I have every expectation that we will be able to pull it together and make the movie."

According to Ford, the anticipation of the DVD release of the *Indiana Jones* trilogy proves the ongoing interest in these movies. 'The reason they continue to have value is their stories. Different cultures tell stories that are intended as cautionary tales, be it

of the Covenant so appealing." A star and a franchise were born. To this day *Raiders of the Lost Ark* is the most successful of the series, generating more than $242 million in U.S. box office, although worldwide the trilogy has grossed $1.21 billion in ticket sales.

"I saw the opportunity to do a character who was instantly attractive to people," remembers Ford. 'The script described something so exciting, and the opportunity to work with Steven Spielberg was undeniable. The whole thing was a major dream. Then we had such a good time doing it."

As it is for nearly every sequel to a beloved original, it was diffi-cult for *Temple of Doom* to live up to expectations. Critics weren't too kind to the second installment and when The Last Crusade came out 1989, Roger Ebert of the Chicago Sun Times concluded:

> " The reason they continue to have value is their stories
> These films are like the Grimm's fairytales of their age. "

Bible lessons, paintings on the wall or stories around a campfire. People need stories for comfort and instruction and to feel part of a cohesive human experience. These films are like the Grimm's fairytales of their age."

Keeping Up With the Joneses

When *Raiders of the Lost Ark* opened in theaters 22 years ago, movie critics were beside themselves: "It's one of the most deliri-ously funny, ingenious and stylish American adventure movies ever made," raved the New York Times, and the BBC called Harrison Ford's performance "most effortlessly charming as the original tomb raider that makes his globetrotting quest for the Ark

"When *Raiders of the Lost Ark* appeared, it defined a new energy level for adventure movies; it was a delirious breakthrough. However, there was no way for Spielberg to top himself, and perhaps it is just as well that *Last Crusade* will indeed be Indy's last film. It would be too sad to see the series grow old and thin, like the James Bond movies."

That was *then*.

Fourteen years have passed since the last Indiana Jones adventure. With sci-fi flicks like *The Matrix* or female-driven action vehicles like *Tomb Raider* or *Charlie's Angels*, the sensibilities of the movie going audience have changed. The consensus in Hollywood is, it doesn't matter that Harrison Ford isn't a spring chicken as long as he ages gracefully and the story of the fourth Indiana Jones film is hip and fresh.

Daredevil stunts have never been Indy's main draw. 'The best scene out of all the films was the one where, when faced with a skilled swordsman, Indy just pulls out his gun and shoots the

The Ford Hero-Meter

Not all heroes are created equal. Some of Harrison Ford's roles are more valiant than others, and occasionally he plays against type. Here's how some of Ford's characters rate:

1977 Star Wars: A New Hope

Han Solo shoots first, demands payment, and doesn't show much hero potential until they very end.

1980 *Star Wars: The Empire Strikes Back*

Solo argues that he's both a scoundrel and a nice man but geats sealed in carbonite for his trouble.

1981 *Raiders of the Lost Ark*

A daring archeologist searches for a Biblical artefact while brandishing a bullwhip. Mixing Brains and charm, Indy is the ultimate hero.

1982 *Blade Runner*

Rick Deckard hunts rogue replicants while his own humanity remains in question.

guy," says media analyst Adam Farasati of Reel Source in a recent *Entertainment Weekly* article. 'The key has always been brains over brawn, and that's given this character longevity that other '80s action heroes like Rambo and Rocky have lacked."

In a time of estrogen-laden action movies, it's possible that a young, female sidekick could take on some demanding stunts in the next Indiana Jones installment. An actress with a marquee value would not only help to bring in an audience of teenage girls, she would also keep up the franchise's history of feisty women like Marion Ravenwood (Karen Allen) in *Raiders of the Lost Ark* and Dr. Elsa Schneider (Alison Doody) in *The Last Crusade*.

George Lucas himself has fueled the rumor-mill with comments that the biggest challenge Dr. Jones might be facing may not involve snakes. 'There is a scene where a lot of Indy's ex-girl-friends show up, but they are not major characters," Lucas told

feeling they have very little effect over their own lives. They think there must be some clue in the lives of people who are successful to help them figure out how to improve their own lives."

The headlines have increased since his current girlfriend, Ally McBeal star Calista Flockhart, moved into his Hollywood Hills home with her two-year-old son Liam and her dog Webster. The couple fueled the fire by recently agreeing to a cover story in

Entertainment Weekly, hinting at cameos by Allen, Doody, or Kate Capshaw (nightclub singer Willie Scott in *Temple of Doom*). Harrison Ford is quoted to have responded with a wink: "It's probably going to be the best scene in the movie."

Romantic Lead

If Indy is in for girl trouble in the next film, Ford will be able to pull from his own experience for the character.

At the age of 60, Harrison Ford suddenly found himself single and dating again. His love life became fodder for the tabloids, a situation to which Ford had not become accustomed, and he says he handles the attention badly. "I'm a target for the paparazzi these days. I don't participate in it, and I certainly don't enjoy it. But as soon as you go out in public, people have the legal right to take your picture." He has his own theory why our society seems to be obsessed with gossip. "I think it has to do with people

1983 *Star Wars: Return of the Jedi*

First he needs rescuing, but then Han Solo helps Luke and Leia rid the galaxy of the Sith.

1984 *Indiana Jones and the Temple of Doom*

Jones saves the children of an Indian village in the series' sophomore outing.

1985 *Witness*

An unarmed John Book overcomes corrupt cops with a speech, and Harrison Ford comes away with an Oscar nomination.

1986 *The Mosquito Coast*

Visionary Allie Fox plans to create his own paradise, but his obsession turns it into hell.

People magazine in which they put their relationship on display. "Romantic love is one of the most exciting and fulfilling kinds of love, and I think there's a potential for it at any stage of your life," says Ford in the article. "I was not surprised that I was able to fall in love, and I wasn't surprised that I did. But I'm very grateful."

Both Ford and Flockhart claim not to be bothered by their 22-year age difference. As a matter of fact, Ford is quick at giving an explanation for the fascination some women have with older men: "Because young men are so goddamn disappointing!" The star who used to be fiercely protective of his privacy, now sees nothing wrong with opening up to the press: "The article and photos in People magazine are really just acknowledging a reality. I'm not embarrassed by it."

Ford and Flockhart met at the 2002 Golden Globe Awards, where-depending on which of them tells the story-she poured a glass of wine over him to get to know him, or he clumsily spilled the wine on himself. "I didn't anticipate anything," he says. "I just met this girl at the Golden Globes, and we got along fine, and we started going out, and all of a sudden we're in a serious relationship. That's the way it happens."

Ford has always been a public figure, but since he got together with another star, the publicity has multiplied, a

> "I like to believe that audiences trust me ...
> They trust the man behind the characters I play"

reality he has learned to live with. "You have to learn to ignore it and do the things that interest you, regardless. And when it comes to the point where you can't go to the zoo anymore, you'll learn to avoid that. Because there are places where you're basically trapped."

Whipping It Up Again

At 61 years old, Ford hasn't lost any of his star power. "I like to believe that audiences trust me" is his analysis of his appeal. "They trust the man behind the characters I play." Years ago he said in another interview that viewers can conclude a lot about him by watching his movies. "Even though each character has certain unique features, I'm not hiding my true self. There's a good part of me in every character I play, and you can learn more about me that way than by my answering a lot of personal questions, where I'm inclined to be evasive."

Unlike his colleagues Robert Redford and Mel Gibson, Ford has no interest in directing. "It takes me five months on a film,"

1989 *Indiana Jones and the Last Crusade*

The Jones boys search for the Holy Grail and find it.

1992 *Patriot Games*

CIA Agent Jack Ryan attack on a member of the royal family while making his own family a target for terrorists.

1993 *The Fugitive*

Dr. Richard Kimble needs to save his own neck before solving his wife's murder.

1994 *Clear and Present Danger*

Jack Ryan fights a South American drug cartel. Holy Smokes!

he says. "It takes the director a year and a half. It's too hard, takes too long, and doesn't pay very well."

After years of success as straightforward heroes like the President of the United States in *Air Force One* or CIA agent Jack Ryan in *Clear and Present Danger*, these parts now seem a bit one-dimensional to him. "I have never been interested in playing a character that didn't have a degree of complication. I've always tried to bring a level of depth to my characters, even when they were meant to be, finally, heroic. I think that's much more interesting than playing the sort of unvarnished hero."

These days, Ford finds most pleasure in comedies. "I love it," he says. "It's where I know the most, feel the most useful, feel the most at home. It's more fun now than it ever was because you feel more experienced every time, more equipped."

You have to consider what an audience is inclined to believe and support."

Harrison Ford has a long and successful career behind him and he feels secure in what he's done up until this point.

"However," he adds, "there are a lot of areas I would like to explore. I'm hopeful that I can push the limits of what audiences expect from me without alienating them. Movies like *What Lies Beneath*, in which I play a villain, or *Random Hearts* presented different opportunities for me, and the variety keeps me interested in the work. I've reached a point where it's important for me to expand my repertoire and I would like to be able to take audiences along with me. It's a challenge." ☙

The one character he certainly is identified with most often is Indiana Jones, and the actor can't wait to put on the fedora again. "It's important to show that he's aged, he's suffered some wear and tear over the years. That's going to make this character that much more interesting. I can't wait to address issues like whether his strength is based on his youth or on other aspects of human nature, like his wisdom, his toughness, his resourcefulness, his integrity. In creating Indy, we gave him a certain history and identity, and I think it will be extremely fascinating to expand on that. It's something that I think the public would enjoy watching."

To him, the question of what is appropriate for Indy has nothing to do with chronological age but with his ability to leap into action. "I'm still quite fit enough to fake it," he smiles. "Paul Newman races cars, even though he's in his seventies. I wouldn't want to pick a fight with a guy like Clint Eastwood, either.

1997 *Air Force One*

President James Marshall fights Russian terrorists himself on his own airplane.

🕊🕊🕊🕊

2000 *What Lies Beneath*

Ford's only turn as a genuine scumbag is Dr. Norman Spencer, who cheats on his wife with a college student played by a supermodel.

🕊

2002 *K-19: The Widowmaker*

Submarine captain Alexei Vostrikov must prevent a nuclear disaster by sacrificing his own crew.

🕊🕊🕊🕊

2003 *Hollywood Homicide*

Police captain Joe Gavilin. moonlights as a real-estate agent but still manages to save the rap community from a killer.

🕊🕊🕊

Below: *Peter Mayhew towers over co-stars Mark Hamill, Carrie Fisher and Harrison Ford in this early publicity still from Star Wars.*

"I'm ,wt musical, I have no artistic license; it was just an opportunity to be in something different."

ROOWA

Twenty minutes after telling George Lucas, "Yeah, we'll give it a go," Peter Mayhew 's life was trans/ormed. The initial jitti,ng for the costume of Chewbacca led to appearances in all three Star Wars. films, and a notoriety that still endures. The man behind the mask talks to Joe Nazzaro.

"I love playing Chewie," says Peter Mayhew. "I think he's got so much more to offer now than he did in the first movie." Mayhew is of course referring to Chewbacca, the towering Wookiee who became - quite literally - one of the most biggest elements of the Star Wars film series. 'They continued to build our characters up, so at the end of *Star Wars*, Chewie is still alive, in the second one, he's one of the good guys, and with the sorting out on Cloud City and everything else, Han and Chewie were synonymous. By the time we did the third movie, he was definitely part of the tradition."

When one meets Peter Mayhew, the first impression is of enormous height. Standing at well over seven feet tall, he seems formidable indeed; his sepulchral voice and shaggy locks contribute to the kind of presence that you wouldn't want to meet in a dark alley. Once you start talking to him, however, Mayhew's twinkling eyes and amiable personality quickly assert themselves, and an almost teddy bear-like quality emerges.

At the time of this interview, Mayhew is a long way from his Norwich home, on the second leg of the aptly-named 'Men Behind the Masks' tour. Here, in a massive New Jersey auditorium, are assembled a number of *Star Wars* luminaries, including Anthony (C-3P0) Daniels, David (Darth Vader) Prowse, Kenny (R2-D2) Baker, Michael (Bib Fortuna) Carter and, of course, Mayhew himself. He's sitting at a table a few yards from the main stage, and from time to time, Mayhew breaks away from the interview at hand to heckle Baker, who's taking questions from the audience.

Most long-time *Star Wars* enthusiasts probably already know the story of how Mayhew had been working as a London hospital porter when he got the call asking to audition for the film. There are actually several different versions of that story (including the one given by make-up designer Stuart Freeborn in Issue 8 of *Star Wars* Magazine) and Mayhew has his own recollection of the incident. "Actually, I had already done Sinbad and the Eye of the Tiger the previous summer, and one of the gentlemen who did all the minotaur make-up was in Elstree [Studios] talking to a production secretary around the same time that Stuart was there doing all the characters for the start of *Star Wars*. At some point in the conversation my name got mentioned, and I got a phone call from this particular young lady. She said: 'Your name has been put forward by a certain person. I hear you're tall; would you be interested in doing a movie?'

"I said, 'Yeah, why not?' having done one, which was a location shoot in Spain for three months. That was great, so I asked her what the part was. She said, 'Well, it's a big hairy creature, and we want to get someone as big as we can possibly get.' I said that was fine, what did I have to do? She said: 'You'll have to come up to the studio and see George,' so I went up there and saw George

Lucas, and that was when I saw the character for the first time. They had a big bit of paper on the wall with all the characters on it, and remembering that she said it was a hairy creature, and the only hairy creature on that particular piece of paper was Chewie.

'Then George came into the office and at that time I'd been sitting down on a chair, so I stood up and his eyes almost popped out of his head. [It was though] his luck had changed for one day and he couldn't believe it, so we had a 20-minute conversation about what I'd done, was I available, did I think I could do it, and I said, 'Yeah, we'll give it a go'. Within 20 minutes, we were on our way down to one of the costurniers to get the costume fitted. It was as simple as that."

Above: In Return of the Jedi, Peter Mayhew's Chewbacca remained an integral part of the line-up. The character's superb make-up had first been designed and applied by Stuart Freeborn in 1976.

RRAGH!

Ironically, for somebody who has become such an important part of the biggest science fiction film series in history, Mayhew insists he had no showbusiness aspirations. 'I'm not musical, I have no artistic license; it was just an opportunity to be in something different. I always reckon if you don't take an opportunity like this when it's presented to you, you're missing out on a hell of a lot, therefore you should go for it. If it doesn't work out, you've lost nothing."

The complicated process of transforming Mayhew into a fanged, furry creature took some time, but the actor didn't mind the discomfort. "I was interested in the process," he explains. "Let's face it, everything you do in life should be interesting and if you don't learn something from day to day, then you've wasted that day. To me, it was a fascinating process, totally different from anything I'd done before, and it was fun, so the deeper I got into the process, the more I enjoyed it."

Like many actors working on an unusual project for the very first time, Mayhew has no difficulty remembering his first day on the *Star Wars* set in 1976. "It was the scene on Docking Bay 94 with Jabba and Han Solo [Harrison Ford], where they consult each other. Jabba was played by an Irishman [Declan Mulholland] - he was digitised later [for the *Star Wars Special Edition*]. That was my first day's shoot, and it will stay in my mind forever and ever, because I was a new boy, a new costume and everything was still strange."

As Mayhew recalls, the role of Chewbacca was initially much

smaller in George Lucas' original script for *Star Wars*. "I'd been talking to Stuart and he originally told me that this particular character would probably be in for a week. We'd have long conversations together while we were building the mask, because I was interested to see how he was doing it, what character he would put on the mask, what it could do, how we could do it, that sort of thing. Stuart said to me that quite honestly, it was a lot of bother for a very short period of time, but obviously when they saw the first couple of weeks' shoots, there was something there - it just worked."

"One of the questions I get asked a lot is 'What was it like, working with Harrison Ford?' and I say it was wonderful, because we were both about the same age, and by the end of the first film, we were both professionals. We both knew what our characters were. You don't do three movies playing closest buddies without some of it rubbing off a little bit. Harrison was quite capable of absorbing all the pressure that came with the later films, and even in the early days."

Like many members of the original *Star Wars* crew, Mayhew had no idea the film would become such a phenomenal success. "Before the movie was released in England, we'd already heard stuff from the States and seen the queues on television but we all thought, 'Oh, that's the Americans for you,' but when it arrived in Europe everyone went bananas.

"Then, when they said, 'Right, we're going to do *The Empire Strikes Back*,' I said, 'Great, same character, why not?' and *Return of the Jedi* was the icing on the cake. By that time, after *Empire*, I thought, 'Forget the work ethic, let's have a holiday!' I took a year off and did virtually nothing - well, I say nothing, but I bought myself a house and redecorated it, so it was something totally different from making movies and wearing strange costumes. At the time, I was really looking for some change in my life, because I was getting older and wanted to do something a bit different."

Looking back at the production of *The Empire Strikes Back*, Mayhew admits there was more pressure the second time around. "However, we were working with the same background crew on all three movies, so it was really only the director that changed. I think that was a good thing, to get someone different who could stamp his own attitude on it. On Empire, Kersh [Irvin Kershner] was a good director, but he literally told you what to do. Well, you learn by your mistakes, and by this time I knew what the character was capable of, so I just went along with it: 'Yeah, okay, you want it done that way? Fine.'

"A typical example of that was the scene where I was welding up on the Falcon wing, and Han comes in and says: 'What are you doing? I'll come up and give you a hand.' That scene was entirely improvised. There was basically no script there, and I was trying to arc weld a piece of plate on the wing which was covered with paint, so if I didn't strike it correctly, the whole plate would have gone up. So Kersh said, 'Do it like that and that,' and the finished product is great."

In fact, Mayhew enjoyed his work with directors of all three films, although for different reasons. "On Jedi, Richard Marquand was a totally different man; he was an actor and therefore understood what we were doing. Like George, he let you do what you wanted to do.

"If George hadn't directed *Star Wars,* the whole thing would have been totally different. George looked at characters and said, 'Yes, it's working, let them go.' We got on pretty well, and I figured if I did anything wrong, George would tell me, but I think you'll find that none of my scenes had to be re-shot, apart from the one with Jabba, which was changed for the re-release. The rest of the scenes are basically in their original form, because that character works very well."

> *"Chewie worked from the moment you first see him in the background, talking to Obi-Wan in the cantina."*

Although some actors may have a little trouble finding the exact performance level for their characters during the early days of filming, Mayhew had no such difficulties with Chewbacca once that suit and mask transformed him into the character. "Chewie worked from the moment you·first see him in the background, talking to Obi-Wan in the cantina. He's looking for a ship, Harrison is sitting over in the comer, okay, come with me, bang bang bang ... the whole scene just worked. That was a good sign, because it foretold a lot of things that were to come. The first couple of weeks on a film is the breaking-in time for everybody; the guys don't know what they want out of special effects, some of the sets were wrong and the camera positions, so you've got to allow at least a couple of weeks for a shake-down period."

One might think the cumbersome-looking costume would lead to some problems on location, particularly where extreme temperatures were concerned, but Mayhew only remembers the locations scenes shot in Norway for *The Empire Strikes Back* as being difficult. "I wasn't actually involved in the Tunisian scenes in Star Wars; so it was only the Hoth scenes, where it was about minus 15 and even with that costume, it was pretty bad. On Jedi, the desert scenes were shot in Yuma [Arizona], and they weren't too bad, because that suit breathes, just like a woollen suit. Every desert normally has a wind blowing across it, so up on the barge, if I turned sideways, the wind blew through the suit, which was lovely, because it kept me cool. It was made out of mohair, and all the little hairs were knitted through the actual sweater and knotted off."

There could have been a few problems filming the forest scenes of Endor in *Return of Jedi*, but Mayhew was warned well ahead of time how to avoid being pulverised by massive redwoods or shot by an enthusiastic hunter. "There are these things they call 'widow-makers', which are branches that have fallen off the trees and come to rest in the lower branches and lodge across the trees," explains Mayhew. "Eventually they rot and drop to the ground from 100 feet. When you're talking about a piece of timber four inches in diameter by eight feet long- well, if it hits you *anywhere* you're going to be dead. We actually had guys on one particular location with shotguns, trying to move these pieces of timber.

"Also, if you look at old footage of Bigfoot, Chewie looks exactly like it from a distance, so I was told not to go anywhere off the set in costume. It was all right if I had the top and a pair of jeans on without the costume, but you can imagine Chewie wandering through this fairly brackenish undergrowth and meeting a hunter. He's seven feet tall - 'It's Bigfoot - bang!'"

After finishing *Return of the Jedi*, Mayhew kept a somewhat lower profile than some of his former co-stars. With a little money in his bank account, he decided to spend his time on a few personal projects. "I moved from London up to Yorkshire, which is a total change of life, because there weren't the conventions and stuff at that particular time. I completely dropped out at·that point. I tried to get an agent and couldn't get one; nobody wanted to know somebody of my size."

So what is Peter Mayhew doing these days? "He's doing conventions. He's enjoying life. We're travelling around, doing conventions all over the US; appearances, signings, whatever is demanded because of the re-releases. It's been wonderful, because you get to meet a lot of people and do a lot of things that as an ordinary guy you would never have thought about doing, so I'm enjoying life, and it's wonderful."

As for the inevitable subject of working on the new Star Wars prequels, the actor says he's definitely available. "If Chewie is involved, or if there was another character, I would be highly delighted to come back. It's the same as with Kenny - at four feet tall, he was perfect for Artoo and I was ideal for Chewie, so end of story, it's come to a nice conclusion."

Nevertheless, one can't help wondering if there still isn't a shortage of talented, seven-foot actors out there, waiting for the next good Wookiee role to come along. "I hope there is," laughs Peter Mayhew, "otherwise I shall be looking for a job!" ☮

Left: George Lucas directs Peter Mayhew on the Death Star set in Star Wars.

Below: Chewie plays along with the deception that allows Luke and Han access to Princess Leia's detention block.

H as this thought ever crossed your mind in the last twenty years of your Star Wars viewing life ... "How come Princess Leia did not present our Galactic Teddy Bear with a medal of honor?"

Chewbacca accepts his medal of honor at the 1997 MTV Movie Awards.

W as the 7'2" Chewie too tall for the petite princess to reach during the ceremony? or ... Was the medal too small and not accommodating enough for such a furry Wookiee? The answer? Simply none of the above. It just wasn't written in the *Star Wars* script.

But that all changed on the night of June 7th 1997 when MTV awarded its "1997 MTV Movie Awards" Lifetime Achievement Honor to none other than Chewbacca.

"I knew the character was popular, but didn't realize that there was that much interest from MTV," says the man behind the mohair and yak-hair mask, Peter Mayhew.

"It was just great to come back home from doing science fiction and comic conventions to a fax from Robin Berlin, Talent Executive at MTV, stating 'We would like you out on certain dates to receive this award as Chewie' and I said 'Yes, thank you very much' and here we are," states Mayhew. "It was nice to be honored in this way." The idea to honor Chewbacca didn't just happen overnight in the Santa Monica offices of MTV Networks. It took a lot of brainstorming and the rediscovery of deeply-held feelings of empathy, for that loveable creature, who was not

let the Wookiee win

CHEWBACCA'S LIFETIME ACHIEVEMENT AWARD *win* BY ATHENA PORTILLO

A proud Wookiee on MTV

As soon as the idea of Chewbacca was mentioned, I thought that's it! It's the least we can do for Chewie 20 years later.

recognized for his efforts in helping the Rebel Alliance destroy the Death Star.

"One of the most asked questions around here is 'Why didn't Chewbacca receive a medal in Star Wars,'" says Rick Austin, Co-Producer of the 1997 MTV Movie Awards.

When the idea of who the recipient was going to be this year circulated around the MTV executive committee table, some of the qualifications that were in mind as a must for a potential winner were the following:

■ Who are the people (or as we can see here, non-human species) that are very popular, in vogue, and runner-ups as favorites of the MTV viewing audience?

■ Who would naturally not be in the running to receive an Oscar or Golden Globe Award anytime in the near future?

■ Who would be comparable to past Lifetime Achievement winners such as Godzilla, Jason Voorhies of Friday the 13th, and The Three Stooges?

"As soon as the idea of Chewbacca was mentioned, I thought, 'That's it! It's the least that we can do for Chewie 20 years later,'" remembers Austin as the furry creature is his favorite character of the Star Wars trilogy.

"We rented the Star Wars movie to see how the medal looked and we took the liberty to design a replica for Chewie, which is different from the usual bucket of gold popcorn that is given to all of our winners," says Austin.

Initially, Harrison Ford was the candidate to introduce the Lifetime Achievement Award to Chewbacca. However, due to a busy work schedule, Mike Myers, host of this year's award show, took over with a speech that made a lot of us think that the award was being given to someone like Robert De Niro.

"It is my great honor to present tonight's Lifetime Achievement Award. This year's honoree has starred in some of the most beloved films of our time and his name has become synonymous with the quiet strength and childlike dignity that his characters convey."

"I know this is a cliched thing to say, but I'm going to say it anyway. This guy is one of the reasons I became an actor ... "

As soon as a scene of Chewbacca on Hoth from The Empire Strikes Back appeared on the big screen behind Myers, screams, laughs, howls and applause filled the Barker Hangar Santa Monica Airport auditorium. Scenes from the Star Wars trilogy and portions from Chewie's "recent appearance" on Larry King Live rolled onward to, surprisingly enough, the thrashing lyrics of ...

"Chewbacca ... What A Wookiee ... "

... from the tribute song by indie rocksters Supernova, which can be found on the Clerks movie soundtrack.

However, once Carly Simon's "Nobody Does it Better " cued on to scenes where our lovable and affectionate Chewie "bear " hugs Luke, Han, and Leia, emotions intensified, as

viewers in the star studded audience remembered how they first came to love this Wookiee.

The tear jerker, though, was not until the ceremonial trumpets awakened our mesmerized senses and Mike Myers said ...

"Ladies and Gentleman, please welcome ... Chewbacca!"

Among the standing ovation crowd, Will Smith and Samuel L. Jackson were the most focused ones in shock and in sheer ecstasy to see the 7 foot plus furry animal walk down the aisle toward them and toward the princess herself, Carrie Fisher.

"I'm so grateful to have worked with Chewbacca,"begins Fisher. "Not just because we both had hair issues-he had too much, and I had two buns-but because he's one of the kindest, gentlest creatures I've ever worked with."

"I only wish we had love scenes."

"So it is my great pleasure and privilege to present this Lifetime Achievement Award to my friend, costar, and giant in this industry ... Chewbacca."

Before that momentous night for Mayhew, (with the exception of the earlier taping of the phony Larry King Live show) Peter had not been in costume since Return of the Jedi.

"It's a strange phenomenon, but when you get used to the costume you sort of know what the character consists of," reminisces Mayhew.

"Chewbacca is a cross between different breeds like a bear or a monkey, therefore, before filming Star Wars, I went down to the zoo and observed the behaviors of gorillas, monkeys, bears, anything big, to see how it moves naturally, and my char acter just came to life."

"In New York for the Larry King taping, I got into char acter with no

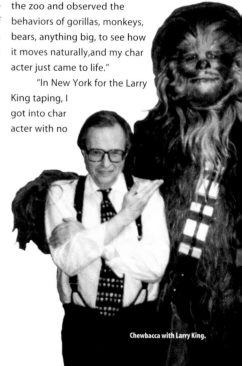

Chewbacca with Larry King.

problem," Mayhew says with a proud gesture."! would be on the set with costume and make-up and before the head went on, I would be talking perfectly normal. Put the head on, Chewie was alive.Take the head off, I would virtually continue the same conversation I was having before Chewie was manifested. I don't know why, it was just one of those things that happened."

Indeed one of those things happened on June 7th as the audience went bananas.

Even Austin didn't know what to do once he came face to face with Chewbacca.

"As soon as I looked into his big blue eyes, I had to walk away because I couldn't believe that I was talking to the real Chewbacca," says Austin in an awestruck fan-like voice. "Peter Mayhew's performance makes Chewie come to life through his eyes, his gestures, just every-thing about him."

Not only had Mayhew not been in costume since Jedi, but he had not seen Carrie Fisher since then as well.

"I've got a date with a princess tonight," sighs Mayhew, with a reddish tinge of blushed shyness, earlier on the evening of the awards taping.

"She's making up for what she didn't do 20 years ago."

"She's going to give the Wookiee a medal," he says."! just know that the whole ceremony is going to be smashing as we are reunited once again. It will be nice to come face to face with Carrie to see how she's grown up and whether she still has that lovely sense of humor which she had when she was 19 years old."

In terms of how Mayhew feels about not getting a medal in *Star Wars* ...

"I say, yeah fine, but I got the last line in the movie because as the camera pulls back you can hear Chewie roaring, so I always think, I was lucky I got the last say."

"But I get my medal tonight," says an ecstatic Mayhew. "It just goes to show that a Wookiee can beat almost anybody, character-wise or personality-wise. Chewie is as good as anybody in this universe and the Star Wars universe."

It seems like Chewbacca got the last say again at the 1997 MTV Movie Awards.

Carrie Fisher seemed to have thought so as well.

After Chewbacca gave his enthralling 30-second speech in his native tongue, Fisher's reply was ...

"I couldn't have said it better myself."

Peter Mayhew with writer Athena Portillo

Chewbacca on *Larry King Live*.

WHAT A WOOKIEE!

HAN SOLO'S OLD PAL CHEWBACCA HAS INSPIRED SOME OF THE MOST VARIED *STAR WARS* COLLECTIBLES AROUND!

WORDS & PICTURES: GUS LOPEZ

Despite missing out on a medal at the Yavin ceremony, Chewbacca is a fan favorite and is represented by hundreds of *Star Wars* collectibles.

[1] One of the most iconic is the tankard designed by Jim Rumpf. As one of the earliest *Star Wars* collectibles, this Chewbacca mug sold by California Originals is said to be one of George Lucas' favorite early *Star Wars* items.

[2] Chewbacca was one of the first four *Star Wars* action figures released as part of Kenner's Early Bird Set in early 1978. Using Kenner's process at the time, which remains largely unchanged to the present day, the original Chewbacca action figure was first sculpted in wax before going through additional stages on its way toward the final model.

The Chewbacca action figure remained unchanged from 1978 through 1985. Kenner updated the card photo during the *Return of the Jedi* release and later bundled Chewie with an aluminum coin for the Power of the Force line.

[3] One of the earliest signs of Wookiee fever was the "Wookies [sic] Need Love Too" bumper sticker. This early sticker showed a common misspelling of Wookiee. A more contemporary version of Wookieemania was this "Flash If You Love Wookies!"

sign used in the 2008 film, *Fanboys*. This misspelled sign appears in one scene and was later corrected in the scene where the fanboys attempt their drive-by antics.

WOOKIES NEED LOVE TOO

[7] Chewbacca also appeared on the Lucasfilm 2001 holiday greetings card as an ambassador for peace in a turbulent year.

[5] For Return of the Jedi, Chewbacca finally appeared on his own Underoos set, a must-have item among well-dressed boys of the 1980s. To complete the Chewie apparel theme, kids could wear these Chewbacca slippers with plastic heads. While Wookiees can tear arms out of sockets when they lose, they also make darn good fuzzy slippers!

[6] Fans were thrilled to see Chewbacca reappear in the Star Wars saga in Revenge of the Sith. Lucasfilm created a special Chewbacca statue as a gift for employees. A more elaborate full body statue in a glass jar was made by Industrial Light & Magic mainly for use as a corporate gift.

[4] To promote food products, Chewbacca would take some unusual forms, including a Kinder Eggs blue hippopotamus and a yellow M&M. The Chewie M&M appeared as different collectibles, including, figurines and plush toys.

Perhaps the best-suited product placement for Chewie was on boxes of "Chewy Choc Chip" muesli bars from Goodman Fielder in New Zealand for Revenge of the Sith. Finally, a product where Chewie promotes something that's actually chewy!

[8] Chewie may have found his calling in collectibles as a cell phone cover. Bundled in a set sold by Orange in the United Kingdom, this Chewbacca cell phone cover with Wookiee fur and bandolier was a stylish way to keep your cell phone warm and safe!

PETER MAYHEW
FANTASY FUZZBALL

The former hospital porter who found fame as a giant, furry space smuggler talks to *Star Wars Insider* about playing the galaxy's favorite fuzzball.

WORDS: MARK NEWBOLD

While there may not be a real mystical energy field that puts the right people in the right place at the right time, fate has famously played a hand in *Star Wars* casting over the years. Indeed, it was one such fortuitous incident—a photograph of 7 foot 3 inches tall Peter Mayhew, printed in a regional newspaper—that led to worldwide fame as Chewbacca the Wookiee.

It was that article, about men with big feet, that set off a chain of events that steered Mayhew away from his job as an orderly at London's King's College Hospital to the door of Andor Films, and their fantasy-adventure movie, *Sinbad and the Eye of the Tiger* (1977). Cast as the towering bronze bull Minoton, the film gave the actor his first experience of working with special effects (under the legendary Ray Harryhausen). The film was a box-office success, but after production wrapped in October 1975, Mayhew returned to his day job at King's College. A year later, a galaxy far, far away pulled him into its orbit, and after an initial meeting with George Lucas, he was cast as the mighty Chewbacca in *Star Wars: A New Hope* (1977).

"I was nervous when I sat down in his office," the actor recalls of that initial meeting and his first impressions of the role. "I had been recommended by a friend to do a part. When George Lucas explained *Star Wars* to me, I thought it was unbelievable. What he created was incredible. I was very excited to have been offered the opportunity."

With the full support of his friends and family, Mayhew took

> **"When George Lucas explained *Star Wars* to me, I thought it was unbelievable. What he created was incredible."**

01 Peter Mayhew on the set of *Star Wars: Revenge of the Sith* (2005).

02 Mayhew (Chewbacca) and Carrie Fisher (Leia) share an off-camera moment during the filming of *Star Wars: The Empire Strikes Back* (1980).

on the role that would eventually define his professional career. However, things could have gone very differently for the actor—and quite possibly the entire franchise—had it not been for another piece of serendipitous timing. Lucas had originally ear-marked the role of Chewbacca for body builder Dave Prowse, but when the actor instead elected to portray Darth Vader (citing that audiences always remember the bad guy), it led to Mayhew's casting as the loyal Wookiee. With each actor having so memorably defined their roles, it's difficult to contemplate them filling the other's boots. "I honestly think it would have changed the

entire film," Mayhew admits, after giving the matter some careful consideration. "I can't imagine how that would've gone."

To help realize his cinematic vision, Lucas and producer Gary Kurtz brought together a crew of technicians and industry veterans, including renowned makeup supervisor Stuart Freeborn, an industry stalwart who played a pivotal part in creating Chewbacca's iconic look. "Stuart did most of the work designing and making it," the actor recalls, reminiscing about the team he worked so closely with. "He knew exactly what we were getting into. He was a master at making costumes under pressure, ▶

▶ and his wife Kay did most of the daily maintenance and grooming. I was honored to work with such a talented crew."

With the role and costume under his bandolier, and Ben Burtt (special dialogue and sound effects designer) assembling a library of Wookiee vocalizations, it was left to Mayhew to figure out how he should bring Chewbacca to life on screen. In search of inspiration for Chewie's unique mannerisms, he took trips to the local zoo to watch the movements of apes, bears, and gorillas, and then worked closely with the film's production crew to put his findings into practice. "The directors and producers gave me most of the direction, usually when we were rehearsing a scene," Mayhew explains. "After that, I made a lot of choices on my own." The end result was a memorable, engaging performance, imbued with the actor's character and spirit now familiar to his legion of fans.

Making Wookiee

When *Star Wars* finally made its North American debut on May 25, 1977, initially in just a handful of theaters, it didn't take long before it had captured the public's attention and rocketed to the top of the box office. Yet despite its exploding popularity both domestically and then across the globe, for many— including some of the cast—the sudden success was unexpected. "It was very surprising," Mayhew agrees, "I honestly didn't know that much about the movie industry at that point. I just tried to do everything that was asked of me. At the time it was a steady pay check, and the rest is history!"

While co-stars Mark Hamill, Carrie Fisher, and Harrison Ford were catapulted into the limelight and became instant household names, Chewbacca's all-encompassing costume afforded

Mayhew relative anonymity, and the actor was able to go about his day-to-day business as normal while he considered his next career move. Despite making a couple of television appearances, it was very much business as before for Mayhew. "I just went back to work at the hospital," he admits. "The film didn't change things that much, but I was grateful to be able to buy a car I could fit inside!"

While *A New Hope* was still raking in dollars at the box office, Lucas had begun work on a sequel, and had made the decision to pass the directorial reins of *Star Wars: The Empire Strikes Back* (1980) to Irvin Kershner. With new hands at the tiller, production of the highly anticipated sequel felt very different

03 Stuart Freeborn adjusts the Chewbacca mask during a costume fitting with Mayhew (seated).

04 Mayhew enjoyed his on-set camaraderie with actors Harrison Ford (Han Solo) and Mark Hamill (Luke Skywalker).

05 Makeup artist Kay Freeborn grooms Chewbacca on the Docking bay 94 set.

06 Han and Chewie escape the Death Star in *Star Wars: A New Hope* (1977).

to its predecessor according to Mayhew, who had been pleased to receive the call to reprise his role.

"There was a difference in style, and everything else," Mayhew remembers of the shoot. "It was Lucas and Gary Kurtz on *A New Hope*, and Kershner and Kurtz on *Empire*." However, for the unassuming actor, the change in

> "Acting in the snow was fine. Rolling in snow made me happy like a puppy."

05

06

THE MAYHEW MAGIC

As the loyal Chewbacca, Mayhew often stole the show on the big screen, but he has also notched up some equally memorable small screen adventures as the wonderful Wookiee:

In 1977 Mayhew made a cameo appearance as Chewie on the *Donnie and Marie* show, followed by a big role in 1978's *Star Wars Holiday Special*. In February 1980 Chewie guest-starred on *The Muppet Show* alongside R2-D2, C-3PO, and Mark Hamill, busting the kind of Wookiee dance moves that only the Muppets can inspire! Chewbacca has also been seen in the comedy short *Return of the Ewok* (1982), the *Glee* episode "Extraordinary Merry Christmas" (2011), and could be seen taking a seat in the original *Star Tours* ride boarding video.

While he may have officially hung up his furry Chewbacca boots, Mayhew remains a big part of the *Star Wars* family as the official Chewbacca Consultant on *Star Wars: The Last Jedi* (2017) and *Solo: A Star Wars Story* (2018), ensuring that future generations will continue to enjoy Chewbacca with a hefty dose of Mayhew magic.

personnel resulted in an enjoyable learning curve. "I was painfully shy back then," he reveals. "All three of my mentors taught me. I was always watching and listening. Kershner was a very hands-on teacher and was always very particular about his instructions. I followed most of them."

The production returned to the familiar stages and corridors of Elstree Studios, but in addition, location shooting meant a trip to Norway and the remote mountain village of Finse, which doubled as ice planet Hoth. It was an opportunity Mayhew relished. "Norway was a wonderful experience, although it created lots of problems for the production, what with the transportation,

shooting, and heating," he recalls. "Acting in the snow was fine. Rolling in snow made me happy like a puppy—but going inside with the snow-covered suit turned me into a heavy, wet mess of fur!" Another box-office hit, the success of the second *Star Wars* outing afforded a financial security that allowed the cautious Mayhew to make a significant life change. "It wasn't until after *Empire* that I quit working at the hospital," he reveals.

Basking in the glow of *The Empire Strikes Back*'s success, production began on *Star Wars: Return of the Jedi* (1983), this time under the helm of new director Richard Marquand. The change in personnel again resulted in the shoot having another fresh

▶ feel. "It was a completely different production without Gary," Mayhew shares. "Richard was an actor, and approached the filming that way. Gary had a much broader perspective on what the final picture needed to be. But really it was just great getting the gang back together."

More Than A Co-Pilot

It's impossible to reflect on Chewbacca's impact upon *Star Wars* without mentioning the relationship at the heart of the character's enduring appeal; the Wookiee's friendship with rogue 'fly boy' Han Solo. It was a connection that stretched beyond celluloid, forming the basis of an enduring comradeship between two actors. "Harrison and I had a relationship like you see on the screen," Mayhew expresses with genuine warmth. "We became good friends, and he was easy to work with. While we only see each other on rare occasions now, we will always have a special bond. *Star Wars* changed our lives forever."

Reflecting on the Wookiee's loyalty to Han through daring escapades, dodgy deals, and the fight against the Empire and the First Order, Mayhew reveals, "It wasn't about the war for Chewie. It was about his friend, who rescued him from the Empire and to whom he owed a life debt. Chewie became Han's conscience, and always wanted to do what was right."

For many, Chewbacca was the heart and soul of the inseparable duo, and Mayhew has his own thoughts on their partnership. "In the early drafts of the story, there was just this one furry smuggler character," he reveals. "Later, George chose to turn that into two parts, so maybe that says it all."

After the original trilogy, Mayhew reprised his famous role in *Star Wars: Revenge of the Sith* (2005), and lent his vocal talents to *The Clone Wars* season three finale episode "Wookiee Hunt," but it was with *Star Wars: The Force Awakens* (2015) that the actor made his swansong as the heroic Chewbacca,

07 Mayhew reprised his role as Chewbacca in *Star Wars: Revenge of the Sith* (2005).

08 Peter Mayhew (top right) with his *Star Wars* co-stars, (left to right) Harrison Ford, Dave Prowse, Carrie Fisher, Kenny Baker, and Mark Hamill.

sharing the role with newcomer Joonas Suotamo, with whom Mayhew was happy to pass on his Wookie know-how.

More than four decades after taking a break from his day job to spend months dressed as a walking carpet, Mayhew is keen to acknowledge the people without whom none of it would have been possible. "The real heroes are the fans," he reflects fondly. "They have kept *Star Wars* and Chewie alive for the last 40 years." ☺

20 REASONS WE LOVE CHEWBACCA

ROLL OUT THE WALKING CARPET! AMY RATCLIFFE PAYS HOMAGE TO A HAIRY HERO...

Chewbacca may not be the most quotable of characters in the *Star Wars* universe, but what he lacks in one-liners he more than makes up for with his heroic actions and emotional growls. Inspired by George Lucas' dog, Indiana, Chewie has been a skilled co-pilot, a fearsome warrior, and, above all, a faithful friend.

His story stretches back to the prequel era and into *The Force Awakens*. Over the decades, he has fought alongside Yoda, Ahsoka Tano, Luke Skywalker, and Rey, but his most constant companion has been his best pal, Han Solo.

Here, in no particular order, are 20 of the reasons to love our favorite Wookiee!

PLAYING PRISONER

Pretending to be a prisoner of the Empire was never going to be Chewie's idea of fun. After all, he had seen his entire planet enslaved by Imperial forces. Still, he went along with Luke's plan to rescue Princess Leia on board the Death Star, and grudgingly allowed himself to be cuffed in binders. Needless to say, the binders weren't locked, and Chewie was able to get back to bashing stormtroopers in no time at all! (*A New Hope*)

THE GREAT ESCAPE

Trapped on a Trandoshan moon with Ahsoka Tano and a group of younglings, Chewie built a transmitter to send a distress message to his nearby homeworld of Kashyyyk. Though his handiwork seemed not to have worked at first, its signal was received by Chewie's fellow Wookiees, and our stranded heroes were rescued by General Tarfful before they could fall prey to Trandoshan hunters. (*Star Wars: The Clone Wars*: "Wookiee Hunt")

FIGHTING PHASMA

When Chewie, Han, and Finn arrived on Starkiller Base, Han assumed that Finn had an iron-clad plan for getting inside and shutting down the shields. In fact, Finn was there simply to track down Rey. Though it was Han that made Finn see how the galaxy was counting on them, and Finn who eventually came up with a plan, it fell to Chewie to play the vital role in the scheme: tackling the heavily armored Captain Phasma. (*The Force Awakens*)

WINNING WAYS

Chewie tried his hand at a game of dejarik against R2-D2 when the *Millennium Falcon* was en route to Alderaan. For all his skill, he was no match for the little droid, and Han had to warn his new friends about Wookiees being bad losers. On hearing that some Wookiees pull people's arms out of their sockets if they don't get their way, C-3PO was moved to offer some of the best ever advice he has ever given, namely, "Let the Wookiee win." (*A New Hope*)

CHEWBACCA VS. DARTH VADER!

Marvel Comics' 2015 *Star Wars* relaunch starts with a confrontation between two *Star Wars* giants as Chewie gets Darth Vader in his sights. While the Wookiee's efforts were ultimately in vain, we wonder how things might have turned out had the Dark Lord been distracted. (*Star Wars* #1 "Skywalker Strikes")

HOLDING OUT FOR HAN

After Lando double-crossed Han, Leia, and Chewie on Cloud City, the Wookiee found himself in binders again—for real this time! As soon as Lando set him free, Chewie was the first to try to punish him, but let him go when it became clear that Lando had a plan to make up for his treachery. Chewie was soon back in his co-pilot's seat with Lando at his side, prepared to play a long game to save his carbonite-encumbered friend. (*The Empire Strikes Back*)

THE GREAT ESCAPE II

As Order 66 cut a terrible swath across the galaxy, Chewie was on hand to help save General Yoda from his own army of clone troopers during the Battle of Kashyyyk. Though Yoda needed no assistance to dispatch Commander Gree and another trooper, it was Chewie who took the tiny Jedi Master onto his shoulder and, alongside General Tarfful, got him to an escape pod and away from the planet. (*Revenge of the Sith*)

HUGGING IT OUT

One of the best examples of the affection Chewie felt for Han came when the two were reunited in Jabba the Hutt's dungeon. Seeing his friend alive and well for the first time since he was encased in carbonite, Chewie swept Han up in a giant Wookiee hug and proceeded to pet his head. If that's not true friendship, what is? (*Return of the Jedi*)

A GROWLING STOMACH

A big Wookiee can't be blamed for having a big appetite, but Han was none too happy when Chewie got the two of them—plus Luke, R2-D2, and C-3PO—caught in an Ewok trap on the forest moon of Endor. OK, when Chewie reached for the booby-trapped hunk of meat he was "thinking with his stomach," but who can't relate to being ravenous and making a dumb decision because of it? (*Return of the Jedi*)

LAUGHING IT UP

No matter how loyal he was to Han, Chewbacca never backed down from giving his best pal grief. When Leia shattered Han's laser-brained delusions in the medical lab on Echo Base, Chewie was quick to voice his amusement with a hearty chuckle. Han gave as good as he got, calling his co-pilot a "fuzzball," but we reckon that a big part of their friendship was based on Chewie being able to keep Han's ego in check. (*The Empire Strikes Back*)

SHARING THE GLORY

Chewbacca played a vital part in the destruction of the first Death Star, yet Princess Leia awarded medals for the victory to Han and Luke alone. Or did she? Not long after the medal ceremony, Chewie found himself fighting the Empire alongside a young woman named Zarro on Andelm IV. He revealed to her that he had received a medal after all—and then awarded it to Zarro in recognition of her own stand against the Empire. What a nice guy! (*Star Wars: Chewbacca #5*)

ALWAYS THE CO-PILOT, NEVER THE CAPTAIN

When Han and Chewie were reunited with the *Millennium Falcon* after many years apart, Han was quick to refer to it as their home. It would have been easy for Chewie to resent the newcomer Rey as she made herself at home in the cockpit, but he was too old and wise to start pulling rank. After the *Falcon* left Starkiller Base without its long-time captain, Chewie stayed in his co-pilot's chair to make way for his new young friend. (*The Force Awakens*)

FRIEND OF ENDOR

Chewbacca didn't get along with the Ewoks at first—which is hardly surprising given that they tried to eat him! But when the Battle of Endor began, Chewie teamed up with his fellow furries to take command of an AT-ST and turn it against the Empire. The combined efforts of Ewok and Wookiee were enough to give the rebels the edge, and ensured that they were able to shut down the second Death Star's shield generator. (*Return of the Jedi*)

SHOWING A SOFTER SIDE

Chewbacca is a towering, intimidating individual with incredible strength, but he isn't afraid to show his delicate side. On board the Death Star, he didn't want to go into the trash compactor because of the smell, causing Han to give him a helpful shove with his boot. And amid the snowy wastes surrounding Starkiller Base, the well-insulated Wookiee had the cheek to complain about being cold! (*A New Hope*, *The Force Awakens*)

GREG RUCKA

STAR WARS

SMUGGLER'S RUN

A HAN SOLO & CHEWBACCA ADVENTURE

A REBEL HEART

After the destruction of the Death Star in the Battle of Yavin, Han thought it was the end of his and Chewie's role in the struggle against the Empire. But Chewie felt as strongly about the Rebellion as he did about his loyalty to Han and the *Millennium Falcon*. So, when Princess Leia called on the pair to stage a rescue mission in the Outer Rim, it was the Wookiee who convinced Han that they had a bigger part to play. (*Star Wars: Smuggler's Run: A Han Solo & Chewbacca Adventure*)

FIRST IN LINE FOR ACTION

When Han needed a command crew for his daring mission to deactivate the shields protecting the second Death Star, Chewie wasted no time becoming the first to volunteer. Though Han said he hadn't wanted to speak for his friend, deep down he must have known he could always count on him. Chewie's own growl dismissing the potential danger seemed to say: "Puh-lease! As if I'm going to let you go without me!" (*Return of the Jedi*)

TO THE RESCUE!

Chewie may feel most comfortable as a co-pilot, but when the occasion calls for it, he's more than capable of flying, err... solo. With Starkiller Base set to explode and Kylo Ren determined to hunt down Rey and Finn before they could escape the blast, it was only the typically nick-of-time appearance of the *Millennium Falcon* that saved the pair. But with no Han to play the hero, it fell to the Wookiee to make the perfectly timed and targeted appearance. (*The Force Awakens*)

A HOME BESIDE THE *FALCON*

Since Wookiees have such long lifespans (Chewie is 234 years old and not quite middle-aged), it isn't such a big deal if they spend a long time away from home. After the fall of the Empire, Kashyyyk became a free world once again, and Chewie returned to the planet to be with his family for a while. Though he eventually went back to his wandering ways, his arrival on his newly liberated homeworld must have been special for all concerned. (*Star Wars: The Force Awakens: The Visual Dictionary*)

GOOD WITH HIS HANDS

When Chewie was imprisoned on Cloud City with a disassembled C-3PO, he did his best to put the protocol droid back together. He didn't get things exactly right as Chewbacca put C-3PO's head on backwards. In his defense, however, Chewie didn't have the owner's manual on hand, plus he had other things to worry about. All that notwithstanding, Chewie *was* kind enough to carry C-3PO's body parts around on his back until he had a chance to rebuild him. (*The Empire Strikes Back*)

WITH BOW OR BLADE

Everyone knows that Chewie is an excellent shot with a bowcaster, and a formidable force with his bare—or rather, furry—hands. But on the "Smuggler's Moon" of Nar Shaddaa, it turned out he was no slouch with a lightsaber, either! Caught in a tight spot with Han and Leia while trying to rescue Luke from the clutches of Grakkus the Hutt, he wielded the unfamiliar weapon with no small skill. Could it be time for a Wookiee Jedi? (*Star Wars #12: "Showdown on the Smuggler's Moon"*)

GOING SOLO
THE SUOTAMO STORY

Chewbacca actor Joonas Suotamo proved a worthy successor to original Wookiee Peter Mayhew in *The Force Awakens* and *The Last Jedi*. Now he's stepping back in time to tell the tale of Chewie's first adventure on the *Millennium Falcon* in *Solo: A Star Wars Story*.

WORDS: DARREN SCOTT

Don't ever listen to anyone who tells you watching movies won't get you anywhere.

"*Star Wars* films were the first movies that I really remember watching," says Joonas Suotamo, who has gone from childhood fan and film student to the dizzy heights of playing Chewbacca on the big screen. "We put on those VHS tapes and I used to wonder about the little details. Like the blue milk that Luke is drinking with his Uncle Owen and Aunt Beru. I didn't know what it was called, but I thought it was porridge, because I used to eat a lot of oatmeal when I was little.

"I also remember watching the gonk droid, and thinking it was a refrigerator with legs, and I completely didn't really realize there was a man inside Chewbacca. I can remember thinking that he was just a bear that they found somewhere."

Suotamo was chosen to be the "bear" for a new generation of fans after nearly five months of auditions for a project called "Foodles"—the working alias for *The Force Awakens*. The process began with him sending a video, filmed by his girlfriend, of his best impression of a caveman. Almost half a year later, following a trip to London to meet J.J. Abrams, he won the role of the world's favorite Wookiee.

"*The Force Awakens* was my first movie, so obviously it was full of those butterflies-in-your-stomach moments, with everything being so new. Getting to work with J.J. Abrams was an experience I will never forget.

"For this new movie," he says, referring to *Solo: A Star Wars Story*, "it was thrilling in a different way,

because working with this ensemble of superstars is such a unique experience. All these movies are their own little world. I can't wait to see this one on screen."

Perhaps the biggest difference this time around is that Peter Mayhew, the man inside the Chewie suit since *A New Hope*, will not be taking part in this latest production. Mayhew and Suotamo shared Wookiee duties on *The Force Awakens*, and the older actor served as a consultant on *The Last Jedi*. Now, for want of a better phrase, Suotamo is going solo.

"Before *The Force Awakens*, Peter and I took part in what we called 'The Wookiee Bootcamp,'" reveals Suotamo. "When we first met, he said I was a little bit too skinny! We spent a couple of weeks together, going into detail about how Peter used to make the suit work for him, the way, for example, that Chewbacca wears his chest proud.

"It was amazing to get that kind of detail, and I couldn't believe how gracious Peter was about it, because it must be hard to see something that you've done all your life be passed on. But I assured him that I had much respect for him and the character he made famous, so Chewie was going to be in good hands. Now I try to take everything that Peter has brought to the role and make it my own, with my own unique physique!"

So how does Suotamo's Chewie differ from Mayhew's now that he is three films in?

"Because of my love for *Star Wars* and all that comes with it, I wanted the Chewbacca that I play to be very similar in essence to the one that Peter plays," he says. "I want there to be that same feeling, when you look at this character in *Solo*, that ▶

PROFILE
JOONAS SUOTAMO

■ Born October 3, 1986 (31 years old)

■ Raised in Espoo, Uusimaa, Finland

■ 6 ft 10 in tall

■ Studied film and video at Penn State University, Pennsylvania, U.S.A., graduating in 2008

■ Played college basketball for Nittany Lions at Penn State, for seven seasons in Finland's basketball leagues, and for the Finnish national basketball team

■ Served in the Finnish military

■ Sold insurance over the phone before landing the part of Chewie

▶ he is thinking about the same things that Peter thought about in the original trilogy.

"It sort of transcends the script and the actor, and it can be very hard to gauge, so I do ask to see my scenes once we've filmed them to be sure I'm doing them justice. Being covered in hair, I don't have the usual references that I do when working with my own face, and I want to do it well. So that's how I approach it."

Being "covered in hair" has other drawbacks, too, and Suotamo describes these as the few "non-perks" of the job. "The suit requires a lot of maintenance," he explains. "Hats off to everyone who works on the suit after each day of sweat and whatever elements we're subjected to while filming, because they have to take such good care of it! If I want to go to the bathroom, we have to remove the entire costume, which takes about 10 minutes. Unfortunately, it takes longer than that to put it back on. It can get very complicated

01 Rian Johnson directs Suotamo in the *Millennium Falcon's* cockpit.

02 Chewie displays his natural charm as a Resistance medic tends to his wounded arm in *The Force Awakens*.

negotiating the filming schedule for the day, but I still wouldn't change it for the world."

Dealing with the elements was, of course, a major issue when filming in Ireland for *The Last Jedi*, where the island of Skellig Michael served as Luke's island on Ahch-To. Here Chewie was reunited with his Jedi friend, as well as making new, feathered pals, in the shape of the lovable porgs.

"I've read the stories that porgs were based on the puffins that were really on the island," says Suotamo, "but I never saw them myself. The actual porgs on set were real enough for me. The creature effects team, guided by the awesome Neal Scanlan, did such a great job in bringing those characters to life. Watching it hop on to the dashboard of the *Millennium Falcon* while we were shooting… It was like a real thing. Of course, I had to forget that there were about five people involved in moving the wings, the feet, the body, the head, and the eyes! It was a big collaboration."

And did Suotamo think of all those people when he had to eat a porg? He laughs. "I've decided now that eating porgs is a very bad thing! And I think that Chewie instantly regrets it, too!"

Not A Piece Of Junk

Speaking of the *Falcon*, *Solo* sees Suotamo stepping inside the iconic ship for the third time. Does it ever stop being cool?

"It is a wonderful place and I could live there," he laughs. "Everything about it is iconic—even the smell! I think Mark Hamill has commented that the smell it had in the 1970s is still there. It must be the glue, or the construction material that they use. I definitely get goosebumps every time we shoot there."

01

"…I completely didn't realize that there was a man inside Chewbacca. I can remember thinking that he was just a bear that they found somewhere."

02

04

05

"I remember the first time I filmed in the cockpit," he admits, "I broke some part of it off! Coming out of that, I tried to be more careful, but the next time I went in, I broke something else entirely. It took me about three tries to get my bearings and not break anything. Shooting *Solo* was great, because other people broke stuff as well!"

Suotamo's enthusiasm for *Solo* is obvious, and not just because he is now the *Star Wars* veteran on the set. "I can't wait to see it, first of all," he enthuses, "because I had such a fun time making it. The cast is just phenomenal. We hung out together; we went to [Qi'ra actor] Emilia Clarke's place. There was me, Donald [Glover, Lando], Alden [Ehrenreich, Han], Woody [Harrelson, Tobias Beckett], and Phoebe [Waller-Bridge, who plays sassy droid L3-37].

"We had such a good time making this film under the guidance of [director] Ron Howard,

who brought so much knowledge and experience to the set. It was just a dream to be making this film. It makes it easier than you might think, being in such good care." He checks himself and chuckles, realizing how excited he sounds.

"Obviously, there's going to be a 'buddy' aspect to this film, where we're going to see how Chewbacca met Han, and how that relationship started. There are a lot of escapades in the underworld, with people who are new and people who are known to us already. It's going to be a fascinating adventure!

"When we were shooting, Alden and I used to make light of the fact that we were both playing these iconic characters. I used to ask Alden to do Harrison Ford impressions, which he can do so well. But I also respected the fact that he wanted to make this character his own, because in acting you sort of have to be careful about not mimicking the character you're playing and ▶

03 Chewbacca's personal makeup team groom his shaggy mane.

04 Chewbacca and Finn (John Boyega) under First Order fire on Takodana.

05 Rey (Daisy Ridley) and Finn join Chewie on the *Millennium Falcon*.

► basing it off someone else's performance. That's what I try to do with Chewbacca and that's what Alden tries to do with Han. It was great to see him give that character his own variety and uniqueness."

Suotamo is, of course, the only actor to appear with both incarnations of Han Solo.

"You're absolutely right! I've never thought of that! I'm very grateful to have worked with both of them. One of them is en route to becoming legendary, and one of them already is. Harrison is everything that I remember watching when I was a kid! Alden saw that, too, I think. He saw the boots that he had to fill and he took it on so well. He was always so prepared. He wrote a lot of notes in the development phase. I can't wait for everyone to see how he pulls it off, because he did such a phenomenal job."

A Wookiee's Story

The title of the movie may be *Solo*, but Suotamo promises that fans will learn a lot about Chewie's background, too.

"It's so interesting, because this movie not only tells the story of how Han and Chewie met, but also things about Chewie's life that we've never seen. When they meet, he's fallen on pretty hard times. I think people are really going to get a new outlook on Chewie after they see that. But it's a buddy movie most of all, and if you've never seen a *Star Wars* film, you can come to this and be totally engaged. You don't need any prior knowledge of this world. It's just a fun-loving adventure for everybody."

People who have never seen a *Star Wars* film? Surely not. Super-fandom is now pretty much the norm! Speaking of which, what has been Suotamo's most memorable experience of *Star Wars* fans so far? He ponders…

"It's either the person who baked me a Chewbacca cake, or the dad in IKEA who wanted to take a picture of me with his two kids. The kids didn't have a clue who I was, so they just cried and tried to get away from me! All the fans are so passionate about *Star Wars*, and they've been there for so long. I feel very humbled that I get to be part of making these stories for the next generation."

As well as a worldwide base of dedicated fans, *Star Wars* also comes with a huge family of cast and crew that a relative newcomer like Suotamo can turn to.

"I feel very lucky to have this experienced

07

08

06 Joonas Suotamo as Chewbacca in *Solo: A Star Wars Story*

07 "U OK, Han?" Chewie lends a reassuring paw to Han Solo (Alden Ehrenreich).

08 Chewbacca (Suotamo), Beckett (Woody Harrelson), Qi'ra (Emilia Clarke), and Han take flight in *Solo: A Star Wars Movie*.

generation of actors who have done it all of their lives," he says. "Anthony Daniels, Mark Hamill, Peter… And also Carrie Fisher, who gave me such amazing advice. I remember when we were flying across the Atlantic for the premiere of *The Force Awakens*, we talked about the fans, and how you need to be in contact with them. She was just so good about that. It's a legacy I'm stepping into."

So, finally, did anyone else have good advice for Suotamo?

"I think I got most of what I needed from Peter and his wife Angie," he says. "They were very helpful in giving me pointers in how to behave. They told me how passionate the fans can be, and how you have to acknowledge that, because they are the reason we're here, basically, and that must be respected.

"It's great that I'm now connected to this character who's so universally known and so iconic. What Peter did in the original films is so personal, and you're very much able to read what Chewbacca is thinking. That was very groundbreaking, I think, for a suited character, and that has a lot to do with why Chewbacca is so loved. I'm just very happy to be part of that. I can't wait for what's next." ☙

"This movie not only tells the story of how Han and Chewie met, but also things about Chewie's life that we've never seen."

HARRISON

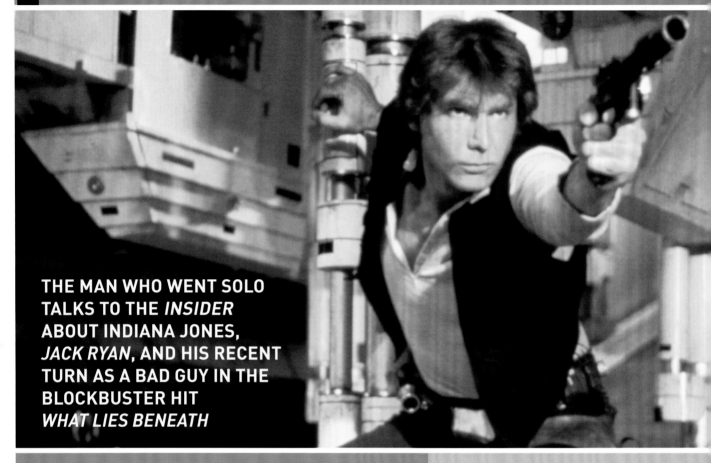

THE MAN WHO WENT SOLO
TALKS TO THE *INSIDER*
ABOUT INDIANA JONES,
JACK RYAN, AND HIS RECENT
TURN AS A BAD GUY IN THE
BLOCKBUSTER HIT
WHAT LIES BENEATH

WHAT LIES AHEAD

WHAT'S THE SECRET to Harrison Ford's considerable success? Maybe it's that, by the 58-year-old actor's own admission, "I never wanted to be a movie star."

He *is* a movie star, of course—he's one of the foremost leading men of his generation in Hollywood and star of some of the most popular movies of all time. But during a July trip to Los Angeles to discuss *What Lies Beneath*, the Robert Zemeckis film in which Ford co-stars with Michelle Pfeiffer, Ford made it clear that he remains ambivalent, at best, about finding himself a superstar.

BY JASON FRY WITH SCOTT CHERNOFF

Harrison Ford as Han Solo takes aim at the Empire in *Star Wars: A New Hope*.

66 I wanted to be a film actor," he said. "I wanted to work in films—I wanted to make a living as an actor doing whatever I needed to do so that I didn't have to be a carpenter or a pizza cook or any of the other things I used to do in order to help make a living. All I ever was ambitious for was regular work of some quality. And I have never really thought through the whole movie-star thing, except that it has always been my ambition from the very beginning to slightly confuse the audience's expectations."

Ford wasn't in town to look back at his past or (alas) to reminisce about *Star Wars*. He was there to talk about *What Lies Beneath*. But in taking the role of Dr. Norman Spencer, the Chicago-born actor has demonstrated beyond all doubt that he doesn't shy away from shocking an audience that thinks it knows what kind of role he likes to play. Throughout his career,

Ford has deliberately tried to confound expectations about him—and with Dr. Spencer, he may have thrown audiences his biggest curve ball yet.

"It's a great part for Harrison—a real departure for him," observed Pfeiffer. "You know, we're not used to seeing him play flawed characters, and I think that will be intriguing for people."

Ford landed in Hollywood in the 1960s and spent time as a contract player with Columbia and Universal, landing bit parts in film fare such as *Dead Heat on a Merry-Go-Round* (he's quickly glimpsed as a bell hop) and *Luv*, as well as turning up as a guest star on such TV shows as *Kung Fu* and *Love, American Style*. But he tired of the routine and became increasingly wary that he was on the verge of being typecast.

So he determined to do things his way: he became a carpenter, working only when he got good parts that he felt would allow him to show his range as an actor. For example, Ford went from playing the arrogant hot rodder Bob Falfa in George Lucas' *American Graffiti* to playing a San Francisco executive in Francis Ford Coppola's *The Conversation*—a pair of roles between which he was the only conceivable link.

Ford's second collaboration with Lucas, *Star Wars*, launched him on a rocket ride to superstardom, but that only made him all the more determined to do things his way. "From the moment I saw *Star Wars*," Ford told the *Insider*, "and realized it was going to be as successful as I thought it was going to be, I determined to do something very different before it came out, so that the audience—or at least the industry—would know that I had other arrows in my quiver and was anxious to fire them as well."

Immediately after *Star Wars*, Ford took a part in *Heroes*, in which he played a Vietnam vet alongside Henry Winkler and Sally Field. He recalled in a 1979 interview that he took the part because he knew it would "show me in something totally different and thus give some proof of my versatility." Being identified

> ## "I NEVER WANTED TO BE A MOVIE STAR."

only with *Star Wars*, he recalled then, "could have been the beginning and the end—with no middle—to my career." He was determined to make it just the beginning, and, as he put it, to "get known first and foremost as an actor, not as that actor who played Han Solo in *Star Wars*."

By the time *The Empire Strikes Back* came out in 1980, Ford had done everything he could to prove his versatility. He'd taken a bit part in Coppola's *Apocalypse Now* as a nameless colonel (he raffishly billed himself as Colonel Lucas), returned to action-adventure in *Force 10 From Navarone*, had his first screen kiss in *Hanover Street*, and played alongside Gene Wilder in *The Frisco Kid*, an Old West road movie matching up Wilder's Polish rabbi with Ford's outlaw.

The paychecks may have increased since then, but the plan has stayed the same. Ford has zigzagged between action movies (the *Star Wars* and Indiana Jones films, as well as two turns as Jack Ryan in *Patriot Games* and *Clear and Present Danger*, and his winning roles in *Air Force One* and *The Fugitive*), dramatic films (*Presumed Innocent*, the sci-fi classic *Blade Runner*, and *Witness*, for which he was nominated for an Academy Award) and comedies (*Six Days Seven Nights*, the remake of *Sabrina*, and *Working Girl*).

But *What Lies Beneath* is something else entirely: a ghost story in which Ford turns out to be decidedly less than a hero. **(A word of warning: If you didn't see *What Lies Beneath* this summer, you may want to stop reading until you do.)**

As *What Lies Beneath* opens, it's been a year since research geneticist Norman Spencer betrayed his wife Claire (Michelle Pfeiffer) by having an affair with Madison Elizabeth Frank (played by model-actress Amber Valletta). Spencer thinks he's gotten away with the affair (and with much more), but then Claire begins hearing mysterious voices and seeing wraith-like manifestations in their New England home. The ghost won't be dismissed; in the end, Claire finds out that her beloved husband is, in fact, a ruthless killer — and one who'll come after her if that's what it takes to keep his secret.

While the bad guy role is certainly different, even for the hard-to-pin-down Ford, he said he wasn't concerned by how audiences might react, calling *What Lies Beneath* an opportunity "to do something different from what people are expecting. This is a different genre than I've set foot in before, but I think it's an especially skillful example of the genre," he said, adding that he was drawn to *What Lies Beneath* not just by the surprising twist the story takes, but by "the quality of truth that I think it has. The relationship between these people is, I think, very truthful—and then it turns to poo, the way things sometimes do."

But Ford said he was drawn more to the script than the menacing character he played. "Ordinarily, I respond to a character and his dilemma," Ford said. "In this case, I responded to the idea of the film itself. It was so immediate, so contemporary. I loved the construction of the script and the surprises built into it, as well as the character."

Zemeckis is an ideal director for Ford—after all, he's hard to pin down himself: he won an Oscar for *Forrest Gump*, but his other films include everything from audience pleasers such as the three *Back to the Future* movies and *Who Framed Roger Rabbit* to the ruminative science-fiction film *Contact* and the edgy comedy *Used Cars*. When Zemeckis was casting *What Lies Beneath* from the screenplay by Clark Gregg (based on a story by Gregg and Sarah Kernochan), Ford was his first and only choice to play Dr. Spencer. The actor quickly agreed to take the role, but couldn't commit to the movie at the time because he was shooting *Random Hearts*. To accommodate him, Zemeckis did an interesting bit of juggling, shooting the first half of the Tom Hanks movie *Cast Away*, then shooting all of *What Lies Beneath* with the same crew, and then reversing course to finish the first movie.

Working with Ford, Zemeckis indicated, made the gymnastics worth it. "The thing that surprised me was how meticulous he is," Zemeckis said. "He wanted to know everything about his character."

Ford noted that he made "a few suggestions" about the script and his geneticist character, noting, "I did a little bit of investigation into genetics and the current state of research and what this character might specifically be doing. As far as the psychology of the character was concerned, I did a little bit of research, but not

TRUST HIM: [Clockwise from obove] manning the *Millennium Falcon*'s defenses in *Star Wars: A New Hope* ; meeting up with Marion in *Raiders of the lost Ark*; and making a point in *The Empire Strikes Back.*

much. I thought I actually understood this character on the basis of what I read in the script."

Ford wasn't just interested in Dr. Spencer's internal makeup. Zemeckis recalled that the actor showed up on the set before he was needed, while the Spencers' house was still under construction: "He was already enmeshed in it. He would say, 'I don't think this character would have a desk like this.' It's wonderful to have somebody doing all that work for you."

Asked about those early set visits, Ford explained that "the house represents the characters, and I was very curious about how my character was being represented. They were shooting scenes in that house before I had a chance to see it, so I rushed right over."

While Zemeckis clearly appreciated Ford's craft, the actor was quick to return the compliment. Asked what makes a successful director, Ford compared Zemeckis to Lucas and Steven Spielberg, citing their "interest in stories, understanding of human nature, our culture—a way of bringing issues which are general and large into a particular forum." He noted that he'd always wanted to work with Zemeckis and admired his "very unique visual capacity. Bob is a spectacular film craftsman and a very skilled storyteller—he is so good that he is able to take a film beyond its genre distinctions, as I think he did with this film." For *What Lies Beneath*, Ford added, "Bob built a number of things in the editing room which were surprises, which were startling."

Ford noted that Zemeckis spent a lot of

> ## "I BELIEVE IN MOVIES—I DON'T BELIEVE IN GHOSTS."

time on production design for *What Lies Beneath*, an attention to detail that would pay off for the actors and for the story: "The bathroom," Ford said, "which there seems to be one of, is in fact one of about six sets, all of them designed for a particular shot to create a certain mood or effect." During shooting, Ford said that Zemeckis used "very long takes, very complicated camera moves. He designed the set for those moves to be possible. And it gave the actors the opportunity to have a much longer run at certain moments, which is very helpful."

It's not surprising, given Ford's no-nonsense approach, that he gave short shrift to any talk of the supernatural. His co-stars mused about the possible existence of psychic phenomena at length, with Pfeiffer recalling an odd experience in a purportedly haunted San Francisco hotel and Diana Scarwid (with whom Ford appeared in *The Possessed*, an eminently forgettable 1977 TV movie) recounting a spooky experience with a Ouija board. But not Ford. Asked if he had ever had a supernatural experience, Ford offered a curt, "No," adding, "I believe in movies—I don't believe in ghosts."

Ford acknowledged wryly that for him, the craft of acting is far more enjoyable than the perks of being a "name" actor—to say nothing of the need to perform star turns to promote a film. But while Ford never wanted to be a movie star, he also isn't going to let that reluctance hurt the pictures to which he devotes so much time and effort. "I take more pleasure in one than the other, but I understand the obligation that we who take the money have to use our access to bring [a film] to people's attention," he said.

While calling acting "just a job," he did acknowledge that his children have had to make some adjustments to having a father who's a household name. But in doing so, he made it clear that his children (he is married to *E.T.* screenwriter Melissa Mathison) have inherited their father's straightforward take on life.

"They certainly have a certain number of people in their lives who they understand to be more interested in the job that I do than might be the case if I were a plumber or a lawyer or something else," Ford said. "There's rather more attention paid to the job that I do, but I think my kids are very strong, independent, developed personalities. I don't think they have any particular taste or utility for my fame." Ford said that so far, none of his children had shown any interest in show business, but added, "I would encourage them to do whatever it is that they want to do."

In addressing his next roles, Ford made it clear he's sticking to his plan of keeping audiences guessing—and isn't shy about keeping critics doing the same. He acknowledged that he passed on *Traffic*, a forthcoming project from director Steven Soderbergh (*Out of Sight*, *The Limey*, *Erin Brockovich*,) but brushed off any speculation that he turned down the movie because his part was another turn as a villain, and therefore too similar to *What Lies Beneath*.

"That didn't work out simply because the character's situation was so grim," Ford said, adding that character (now being played by Michael Douglas) is not really a villain but rather dealing with serious problems. "His daughter is a drug addict, and I didn't want to spend another two hours on-screen being grim about something after *Random Hearts*, in which I had a similar dramatic obligation. I thought I didn't want to bring that kind of character to the audience again without doing something else in between."

That being said, Ford put the kibosh on rumors that he felt he might "need" to do an action picture next, observing, "I don't make these announcements—I don't know where this stuff comes from." He did note, however, that "I have fun rolling around on the floor with the stunt guys. And it's interesting to try and develop a story in action sequences."

Could that mean another turn as the intrepid archaeologist Indiana Jones could be on tap? Well, maybe. Although Ford made it clear that rumors making the rounds about a fourth movie in the series dreamed up by Lucas and Spielberg are so far exaggerated, he didn't close the door on the possibility.

"The reason people are still asking is because we're still saying that we all want to do it," Ford said. "It's simply a matter of finding a script that we all agree upon, that we're equally enthusiastic about, and finding a time when we can all three work together." But, he added, no such script has been written yet.

On the other hand, Ford firmly shut the door on another outing as as Jack Ryan, the character Ford played in adaptations of two Tom Clancy novels. The actor said it was "not likely" he would take the role again in *The Sum of All Fears*. "I passed on the last script," he said, "so I think that puts an end to it." (Fans who remember that Ford took over the role from Alec Baldwin will observe that Ford's decision only puts an end to *his* involvement—in fact, Ben Affleck is in discussions to become the third Jack Ryan.)

So what's next for Harrison Ford, who's played everything from bell hop to U.S. President, spice smuggler to research geneticist? Will it be an action-adventure, a romantic comedy, a drama or even another turn as a villain? Or could another Indiana Jones adventure lie ahead? It's anybody's guess, but as anyone who's watched his career for any amount of time knows, Harrison Ford's next role will be one that speaks to him not as a movie star, but as the only thing he's ever wanted to be: an actor. ☙

> ## "I HAVE FUN ROLLING AROUND ON THE FLOOR WITH STUNT GUYS."

the beginning, there was only one book: Star Wars by George Lucas. It would be years before the exp

universe exploded into the broader public consciousness, but along the way, one author would consistent

depth to the characters and situations Lucas had set in motion. As much as any author currently working in the Star Wars un

Brian Daley left his permanent mark on it with his Han Solo adventures and his radio dramatizations of all three films, the first of

continues to rank as one of National Public Radio's highest-rated dramas of all time.

REMEMBERIN
BRIAN DALE!

by Michael G. R

If you've been a *Star Wars* fan long enough, you may well remember the first time you encountered the work of the late author Brian Daley: in early 1979, *Han Solo at Stars' End* became only the second novel (following Alan Dean Foster's *Splinter of the Mind's Eye*) to continue telling tales in George Lucas's mythic galaxy. Unlike *Splinter*, which followed Luke and Leia in a post-*Star Wars* adventure, *Han Solo at Stars' End* went back in time to chart the Corellian smuggler's escapades in the days before he first encountered Luke Skywalker and Ben Kenobi in the Mos Eisley cantina. Two more books would follow (*Han Solo's Revenge* and *Han Solo and the Lost Legacy*), putting Brian Daley on the map as one of readers' all-time favourite authors to expand the *Star Wars* universe. This from a man who had been a house painter, a welfare-case worker, a bartender, a loading-dock worker, a self-proclaimed "bum," and a waiter in his earlier, leaner days, a man whose claim to fame in 1979 was a pair of moderately successful fantasy novels. Now, over 20 years later, one of Brian's best friends, James Luceno, is well on his way to becoming a noted *Star Wars* author himself, with his *Cloak of Deception*, *Agents of Chaos* duology, and the e-book *Darth Maul: Saboteur* continuing to build on a galaxy his friend introduced to him back in the late 1970s. The two men would eventually pen nearly the entire *Robotech* series together.

"When we met, we were both dating women who were working as wai in the same restaurant in New Jersey," James recalls. "And we were both w on our first novels. The two women had become friends, and inevitabl both realised they were dating writers."

Brian was working on his first fantasy novel (*The Doomfarers of Cora* 1977), which chronicles the exploits of a squad of soldiers during the Vietna who find themselves mysteriously transported to a world of sword-and-s there, they must slay a dragon to return to the real world once again. The bo sufficiently popular to spawn a sequel (*The Starfollowers of Coramonde*, 197 the two books made Brian Daley one of the lead authors for Del Rey, an im the great publishing house Ballantine. (Another of Del Rey's heavy-hitting a at the time was Terry Brooks, who would eventually write the novelization *Phantom Menace*.) When the license for *Star Wars* came Del Rey's way, Bri the first author the publishers considered, weighing not only his writing st successes but also what they considered his ability to "click" with the *Sto* characters. Brian himself couldn't have been more enthusiastic - he had se *Wars* with James Luceno, and from "the minute Brian saw that movie, his wh changed. He was just enthralled by the vision that George Lucas offered. In ways, it was very close to what he was trying to do in his own fiction."

"HE WAS VERY DEDICATED TO THE TRILOGY, TO THE MYTHOS BEHIND THE AND TO THE MESSAGE OF THE STORIES THEMSELVES," – EDITOR SUE RO

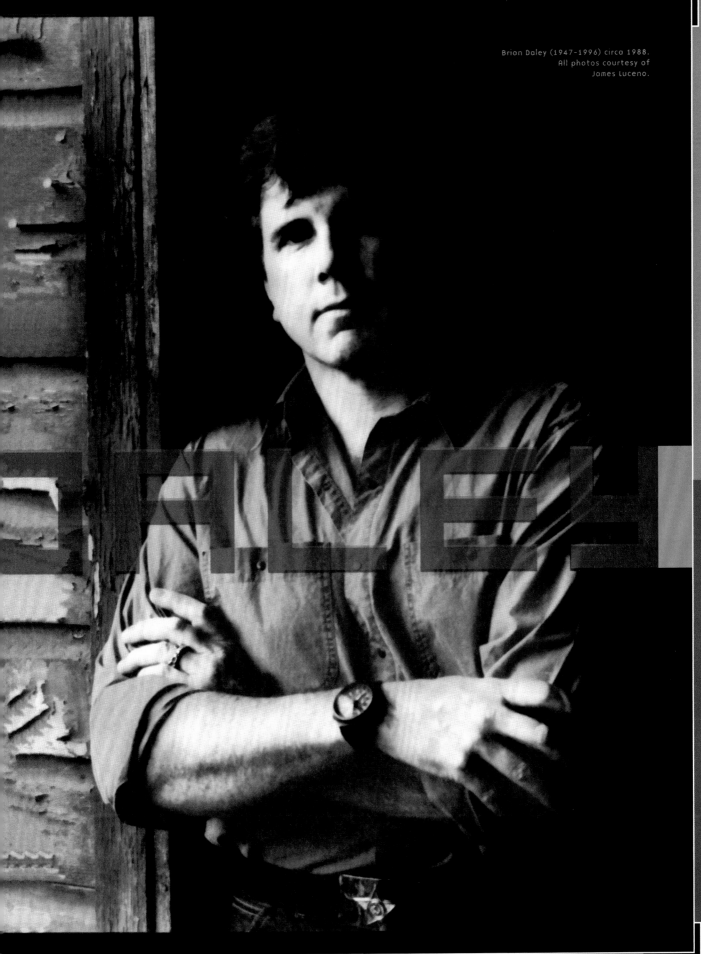

Brian Daley (1947-1996) circa 1988.
All photos courtesy of
James Luceno.

Brian, in 1981, at the Los Angeles recording of the first *Star Wars* radio drama, for National Public Radio.

Initially, both Lucasfilm and Del Rey believed the books were going to be a trilogy about Luke Skywalker, James points out, adding, "At that point, no one knew the film was going to become such a phenomenon." In the end, however, Lucas decided to preserve his central character for the screen and focus the fiction instead on one of the supporting players in his mythos, Han Solo. This was perfect for Brian Daley, who bore some personality traits similar to Solo, not the least of which was the clever comeback. According to James Luceno, Brian "could've been a standup comic if he'd wanted to be." Furthermore, he had a very easy-going style like Han's and was something of a romantic at heart, both of which allowed him to soften some of Han's rougher, mercenary edges. Despite Brian's quick affinity for the character, there were still continuity issues to consider. "Brian's original outline called for Han doing things within the Empire," James notes, "but Lucasfilm rejected that because they weren't sure what they were going to do in the second movie. So, they wanted Brian to set those books in a different part of the galaxy, someplace that wouldn't break any of the continuity that might be established by the films."

Thus was born the Corporate Sector Authority and their stormtrooper-wannabes, the Security Police (or Espos, for short). The Empire gets a brief mention

to give the reader a perspective of the galaxy, and from then on, Brian's trilogy stays firmly rooted in previously unexplored branches of the *Star Wars* universe. (A.C. Crispin's final book in her Han Solo trilogy, *Rebel Dawn*, does a fine job of explaining how Han ended up in the Corporate Sector in the first place – to avoid getting married – and accounts for some of the gaps between Brian's books.) In addition to the continuity restrictions, Brian found himself up against an even more demanding barrier: time. He had six weeks to produce the first Han Solo book.

"Brian could be very, very fast," James Luceno says. "We had very different writing styles. Brian would sit down at a typewriter – he used a manual typewriter – and he would just hit those keys steadily for four hours where I sort of write a couple of lines, then sit back and think about it for a while. But then again, the last books he wrote in his life, a series that was finally called *Gammalaw*, he worked on for 10 years. He would do it however he needed to." James found himself serving as a sounding board for *Han Solo at Stars' End* during those rushed weeks, and not long thereafter, both authors found themselves with new books on the shelves. (James Luceno's book *Headhunters*, the book he'd been working on when he first met Brian Daley years earlier, was published in 1979 as well.)

AT STARS' END

Brian's Han Solo trilogy was not only well received by the public (who, after an initial bit of surprise – *Splinter of the Mind's Eye* from 1978 had given the impression that all adventures to follow would, indeed, *follow* the original film – embraced the books with much enthusiasm), but by Lucasfilm as well. The third book wasn't even on the shelves yet when, in 1979, Carol Titleman of Lucasfilm hired Brian to write the script for the *Star Wars* dramatization for National Public Radio. As the vice president in charge of overseeing the project, Titleman choose Brian to draft the radio play from late 1979 until mid-March of 1980 because she could see his deft handling of the Han Solo character and his general feel for the *Star Wars* universe in his trilogy. Those 13 half-hour episodes quickly became something unique: While retelling the by-then well-known tale of the original film, they "filled in" dozens of scenes that took place in between the established familiar moments, opening up the movie a bit. Simple throwaway lines from the film – Vader to Leia after capturing her, "You weren't on any mercy mission this time" – suddenly became significant moments in the unfolding tale, backstory that had finally made it the forefront. (Interestingly enough, a scene that was restored to the film for its rerelease, one between Han and Jabba the Hutt, appears in the radio drama as a confrontation between Han and one of Jabba's hired thugs named Heater.) In June of 1980, Brian joined the voice cast (including Mark Hamill as Luke and Anthony Daniels as See-Threepio) in Los Angeles for two weeks of recording. Brian's job: to write "wild lines," bits of dialogue murmured and muttered by background characters in crowd scenes, lines that can be ad-libbed in most radio drama but which required special attention in the *Star Wars* universe. Furthermore, some lines that read well on paper sometimes didn't come out quite as well when voice actors were speaking them. Thus, Brian

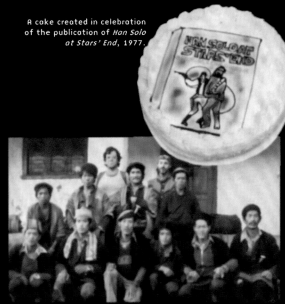

A cake created in celebration of the publication of *Han Solo at Stars' End*, 1977.

[ABOVE] Brian and Jim Luceno, with Nepalese porters, 1983. [BELOW] From left to right: Brian Daley, Jim Luceno, Chris Barbieri, and photographer Joel Simon, in Guatemala, 1994. Chris is the illustrator who created the maps for the *New Jedi Order* series.

DALEY AFFIRMATION

The cast and crew of the final radio dramatization, *Return of the Jedi*, made a point of recording a special message for Brian, each of them taking their hand at adding a line or two to make the tape truly a shared venture. Perry King (Han Solo) and Ann Sachs (Leia) were joined by Josh Fardon (replacing Mark Hamill from the first two radio dramas as Luke), Brock Peters (Darth Vader), Paul Hecht (the Emperor), Edward Asner (Jabba), and even director John Madden and special effects wiz Tom Voegeli to send a short message to Brian, telling him how much he was missed and appreciated. And of course, the inimitable Anthony Daniels returned once more as See-Threepio, giving Brian's tape that unique touch that will forever be the voice of a galaxy far, far away…

(MUSIC: STAR WARS THEME CRASHES IN. HOLD & FADE UNDER)

LIVELY CROWD: From the Rebel Alliance, Brian. We wish you were here. *(LOUD CHEERS AND CATCALLS)* *(CHANTING)* Bri-an. Bri-an. Bri-an. Bri-an. Bri-an. Bri-an. *(FADING UNDER AS MUSIC FADES UP & HOLDS)*

(MUSIC FADES UNDER)

LEIA: *(URGENTLY)* This is Princess Leia Organa transmitting to Brian Daley on Earth. We seem to be having a bit of a time warp here. Luke seems to be shedding years as he matures into a Jedi Knight and…

HAN: *(INTERRUPTING)* Leia?

LEIA: Han?

HAN: Are you talking to Brian?

LEIA: Uhhuh.

HAN: You… You love him, don't you?

LEIA: *(LONG PAUSE)* Well, yes.

HAN: *(PAUSE)* Fine. I understand. When he comes back, I won't get in your way.

LEIA: Han, he's the *writer*.

HAN: The writer! Then you weren't… well… but then, Brian isn't…?

LEIA: *(INTERRUPTING)* Why don't you just stop worrying about Brian and… kiss me.

HAN: Uh Leia. Uhhh. *(HE KISSES THE BACK OF HIS HAND WITH ARDOUR)*

LEIA: Uhh mhhh. Urgh! Aggh! *(GRUNTING & SWEATING FX) (JABBA MUSIC FADES UP UNDER)* Get that tongue off me! You vile-*thing*, you! *(SHE LAUGHS, UNABLE TO CONTAIN HER MIRTH ANY LONGER. A REAL PRO.)*

PERRY: *(LAUGHING)* Hey Brian!

PERRY & ANNE: We love you. And we miss you.

JOHN MADDEN: *(ECHOING, AS IF FROM A GALAXY FAR, FAR AWAY)* We miss youuuu…

(MUSIC GETS MORE SINISTER) (FADE UP PALACE CROWD ATMOS) (DISGUSTING NOISES)

JABBA: Yabrianndaley gomm-makikochh. Ggehhht welllll. *(HE FALLS ASLEEP, SNORING)*

SALACIOUS CRUMB: *(CACKLES WITH HYSTERICAL MIRTH)*

(PALACE FADES UNDER AS MUSIC CROSS FADES TO BATTLE THEME)

R2: *(EMERGENCY WHOOPS)*

LUKE: Artoo. Prepare to lay a course on the navicomputer.

R2: ??*!!?

LUKE: What? My part?

R2: !

LUKE: No, it's fine. I just took over for another actor.

R2: *??

LUKE: No, it doesn't hurt. I won't let it. Okay. Course plotted. Get ready to jump into hyperspace.

R2: **?

LUKE: That's right. We're going to go to the Baltimore system. I have a promise to keep - to an old friend. Look, actually, I've never met the guy. But do you think I'm going to pass up an opportunity like this… *(PROXIMITY ALERT STARS SPEEDING UP)*

JOHN MADDEN: *(INTERRUPTING)* Okay. Okay. *(CUT FX)* I just want to do one pickup, Tom. Can we just go please from… "Your mother's a set of matched luggage." Stand by. *(LAUGHS)* Hi, Brian… *(LAUGHS. HE CAN'T GO ON. ANOTHER REAL PRO.)* Ok. Cut. Thanks.

TOM: *(OVER TALKBACK) (LAUGHING)* Great!

>>CONTINUED ON NEXT PAGE

STAR WARS
EXCLUSIVELY ON PUBLIC RADIO

FROM A GALAXY FAR, FAR AWAY…
THE BIGGEST BOX OFFICE HIT IN MOVIE HISTORY IS NOW A STUNNING STEREO RADIO EXPERIENCE.
LISTEN TO THE ADVENTURES OF LUKE SKYWALKER AS HE AND HIS FRIENDS CONFRONT THE EMPIRE IN 13 EXCITING EPISODES.
EXCLUSIVELY ON NATIONAL PUBLIC RADIO STATIONS NATIONWIDE.

was always present on the sidelines, changing the lines so they worked well, or writing wild lines. In his introduction to the published radio play in 1994 (Del Rey), Daley describes his involvement in the process as "frenetic at times, but I've seldom enjoyed myself more." He was present for all the recordings for *Star Wars* and *The Empire Strikes Back*. Only during the recording of *Return of the Jedi* did Brian have to work from a distance - because by then, he was dying of pancreatic cancer. The timing could not have been more profound; originally, it had looked as if, despite the amazing success of the first two radio plays, *Return of the Jedi* might never happen.

"They were originally going to adapt the last film in 1983," James Luceno remembers. "We'd just got out of a 30-day trek in Nepal, in the Himalayas, and when we came back to Kathmandu, there was a telegram waiting for Brian. 'They've decided they want to do *Jedi*,' it said. 'And they want you to do the dramatization.' He was very excited. Then the funding just fell through after we came back to the States. [NPR had had financing problems.] It was something he wanted to do in all the years that followed - he wanted closure, he wanted to be responsible for having done all three films. When he fell sick with cancer, not a month after he was diagnosed, they began to pursue it again." Nearly 10 years had passed between *Empire* and *Jedi*.

When NPR finally found the money for the ROTJ budget, Brian's involvement as the writer of the scripts was instrumental in convincing Anthony Daniels to return to reprise his role as See-Threepio. Daniels felt that Brian "had a real ability to capture Threepio's strange mixture of humourless comedy, his oddly bleak but loving

[FACING] The original poster advertising the first *Star Wars* radio dramatization. [ABOVE] Each installment's script is available in a trade paperback, audio CD, or cassette.

(VADER THEME SMASHES IN. VADER BREATHES UP CLOSE)

VADER: Greetings, Brian. I kneel before you and await your orders to execute your wish. *(FADE BREATHING & MUSIC UNDER)*

BROCK: *(CONTINUING)* Brian, this is Brock... Get well... Rejoin us, soon... Love...

(FADE UP EMPEROR'S THEME & HOLD UNDER)

EMPEROR: *(CHILLING ACOUSTIC)* Brian... Your overlord the Emperor is pleased... with his lines, and commands you to get well, be well, to stay well...

(FADE MUSIC)

(ECHOING ATMOS)

R2: *** ** *

(SERVO MOTORS APPROACHING)

3PO: *(CALLING)* Artoo? Artoo-Detoo? What you doing here, in an empty studio?

R2: ** ** * *** *

3PO: Rehearsing for your next scene? But Artoo, we have finished recording *Return of the Jedi*.

R2: ***

3PO: Oh don't be sad, Artoo. We had a lot of fun, didn't we? And all because of Master Brian.

R2: *** ***

3PO: Yes. I think he did an *excellent* job. But... well... I think he gave you rather too many lines.

R2: !

3PO: Just you watch your language!

R2: ** *** **!

3PO: Ohh. That is a good idea, Artoo. Um, let me see. Um, um. *(TAPS THE MICROPHONE TENTATIVELY)* Hello? Um.

R2: **

3PO: Um. Ready? *(CONFIDENTLY)* Master Brian. Artoo and I want to say that it has been a distinct honour and a *joy* to work with you.

R2: **

3PO: With our thanks, we send you our very *best* wishes. *(PAUSES. THEN TO ARTOO)* There!

R2: ***??

3PO: No, you can't have another retake, Artoo! Oh really! *(HIS VOICE FADES AS THEY LEAVE)* The trouble with you is, Hollywood has affected your circuits. You have become ridiculously starstru... *(A DISTANT DOOR CLOSES BEHIND THEM)*

(SILENCE)

---

personality. No other writer has been able to do this for Threepio, outside his movie incarnation. Only Brian, at the end of the Ewok storytelling scene, could find a radio way of capturing the droid's deeply felt frustration with Han Solo." With Brian on board – though his illness prevented him from being present in Los Angeles for the recording of the six chapters of *Jedi* – Daniels felt that the final chapter of the *Star Wars* radio saga was in good hands.

"I talked to him on the phone many times during his work on *Jedi*," says Sue Rostoni, an editor at Lucas Licensing; she served as Brian's editor in 1995 as he developed that final script. "His timeframe to work on this was pretty short, so whenever he needed information, he called me. He struck me as a very warm man, very much into *Star Wars*. There were parts of himself that he brought to the *Return of the Jedi* script that wouldn't have been there if someone else had worked on it."

While Brian's illness was not a secret, he maintained an impressive level of professionalism during the process of writing and rewriting, focusing not on the severity of his illness but on the writing at hand. "I think it kept him alive those last few weeks or months," Sue says. "It was very, very important to him that this be done. He was calm but energetic, very present – he didn't even sound ill. In fact, we didn't even talk about his illness; we just talked about *Star Wars*. He talked often about what it brought to him."

In the end, it was as much about what Brian brought to *Star Wars* as what it brought to him; the cast and crew of the radio dramas held him in the highest regard, and his presence and skills were sorely missed at the recording of the final instalment of the radio trilogy. Anthony Daniels describes, in his introduction to the published *Return of the Jedi* radio dramatization (Del Rey), how Brian was kept apprised of progress via daily telephone calls, but more important, how the cast convened on the last Saturday of recording to prepare a special tape for Brian, one that conveyed their appreciation for his talents and their affection for and admiration of the man who possessed them. As Daniels says, "The finished tape would be sent to Brian as our way of saying 'You were with us all the way.'" (See sidebar for the complete transcript of that special tape.) Regrettably, Brian would never hear the finished tape, completed on that last day of recording - he died that March night in 1996, in his home in Arnold, Maryland. His longtime companion, historical novelist Lucia St. Clair Robson, was with him. He was 48 years old. He'd been a full-time writer for nearly 20 years, almost since *Star Wars* itself began.

Jim Luceno, Chris Barbieri, and Brian Daley, atop Temple I in Nakbe, Guatemala, 1994.

A WIND TO SHAKE THE STARS

As James Luceno's books in the *Star Wars* universe begin to generate their own fan following, he is quick to point out that he owes a great debt to Brian Daley for introducing him to science fiction in the first place. "The books I used to write were adventure novels set in different parts of the world," he says. "But Brian was doing some script work for an animated TV series called 'The Adventures of the Galaxy Rangers,' and he basically browbeat me into joining him in working on that. I had no confidence that I could do it, but we each ended up writing seven scripts for that series. Then, shortly after the series ended, *Robotech* came along, and Del Rey had the license to the *Robotech* series. They knew we'd worked together already, and they wanted us to join up again. As a result, we ended up doing quite a few projects together, including *The Black Hole Travel Agency* series. More important, we'd been talking about *Star Wars* a lot, because frankly, we thought that *we* were going to write those early novels that restarted the universe...."

In addition to the *Robotech* and *Black Hole Travel Agency* books (all of which were published under Brian's pen name, Jack McKinney), Brian wrote many other science fiction and fantasy novels during his career – *A Tapestry of Magics* (1983), the novelization for the film *Tron* (1982), the Floyt and Fitzhugh trilogy (1985-87), for example. But he will be best remembered for his contributions to the *Star Wars* universe, a universe that was virtually unexplored when he began to chronicle Han Solo's exploits. Under slightly different circumstances, he might have still been chronicling those adventures when the expanded universe plan took off in earnest in 1991 with Timothy Zahn's *Heir to the Empire*. Del Rey, the Ballantine imprint for which Brian had penned the Han Solo trilogy, had retained the license to *Star Wars* novels, and Brian was tapped to write those first books that would relaunch the *Star Wars* universe. Unfortunately, an apparent internal political battle at Ballantine led to the loss of the license, so despite the publisher's intentions to use both Brian and James Luceno to write

the new novels, the universe began again under Bantam and Timothy Zahn's vision. "He'd done a lot of thinking about what he wanted to write in the universe," James Luceno says of Brian's preparations to write more *Star Wars* novels. "He would've tried to give it more of a mythological tone. I'm a fan of Tim Zahn's work, and I think the difference would've been that it wouldn't have been military science fiction, but more of the mythical fantasy that Lucas demonstrated in the films. More quests, more about the Jedi Knights. Have Luke put together a sort of Knights of the Round Table, which Bantam eventually did anyway."

James concedes that Brian wasn't much of a fan of the approach that Bantam eventually took, though in time he might've come around. "He felt that the expanded universe had gone off course," he says. "I think he would've been much happier if he had been around to see it go the way of The New Jedi Order. He would've wanted to see more of a serialized expansion of that universe, not in bits and pieces, falling back and filling in parts. Something that would move steadily forward, as The New Jedi Order does. He would've liked that."

Brian's Han Solo trilogy and all three of his radio dramatizations have been reprinted in recent years, the former as both individual books and a single volume, a steady reminder of his contribution to George Lucas's ever-growing universe. Instead of seeming quaint, his Han Solo books have instead become iconic, adding terminology and technology that are still used in the *Star Wars* worlds (the swoop bikes from *Han Solo's Revenge*, for example, predated *Return of the Jedi*'s speeder bikes by a good four years). And the radio dramas sold astonishingly well when released on CD a few years ago.

"He was very dedicated to the trilogy, to the mythos behind the stories, and to the message of the stories themselves," editor Sue Rostoni says of Brian Daley. "It seemed like it was part of him, and in the same way, he'll always be a part of *Star Wars*."

SOLO
RETURNS

GOING SOMEWHERE, SOLO? THE *STAR WARS* UNIVERSE ISN'T
FINISHED WITH YOU JUST YET! THERE'S A WHOLE NEW RACE TO
RUN IN THE *HAN SOLO* MINISERIES FROM MARVEL COMICS, AS
SERIES EDITOR JORDAN D. WHITE TELLS
MICHAEL KOGGE...

Wahoo! Han Solo takes the controls of the *Millennium Falcon* ! Interior art by Mark Brooks.

Reports of Han Solo's demise have been greatly exaggerated. This summer, the smart-mouthed scoundrel returns for a five-issue Marvel Comics miniseries all his own. *Han Solo* takes place between *Star Wars* and *The Empire Strikes Back*, when Han is still deciding whether or not to throw his remaining chips in with the Rebel Alliance. Written by Marjorie Liu (*X-23, Monstress*) and drawn by Mark Brooks (*Cable & Deadpool, Ultimate X-Men*), it tells the story of Han's entry into daredevil starship race the Dragon Void Run. Yet there's more at stake than just a reward. Her Royal Highness herself, Princess Leia, is using the race as cover for a top secret rebel mission. *Star Wars Insider* met Marvel Comics editor Jordan D. White at the starting line to find out more.

Star Wars Insider: Why did you want to do a Han Solo series?
Jordan White: "Because he is awesome," is the clear answer. Han was a top priority for us ever since we started working on *Star Wars*, and it was more a matter of "When?" than "Why?" We just needed to make sure we had the right creators and the right story in place. He's so likeable, he's so charming, and he's such a key ingredient in the recipe for that original film. Imagine if Luke and Ben had chartered a flight with a run-of-the-mill space captain. How much less fun is *that* movie?

So why now?
I wanted Marjorie Liu to work on *Star Wars* for a while. I'd read the work she had done on *X-Men* and thought she would be a great fit and an exciting voice for the far away galaxy. I spoke with her, and when I heard how excited she was to make it happen, I knew it was the right time. She pitched us a number of great story ideas for a variety of characters, but it was this Han Solo one that really resonated with [Lucasfilm's] Story Group. Her pitch for *Han Solo* as essentially *The Cannonball Run* in space was right on the mark. I also thought it was about time we had Mark Brooks back working on interior art. Mark's solely been doing covers for the last few years, including many for our *Star Wars* series. I cannot tell you how excited I am to have him doing the art for this series. When you look at the detail he has put into every page, you can see his enormous passion for *Star Wars*. It's a real labor of love.

What's the narrative arc of the series?
What runs throughout the story is the pull between Han's old life as a rogue and scoundrel, and his new life with his friends

137

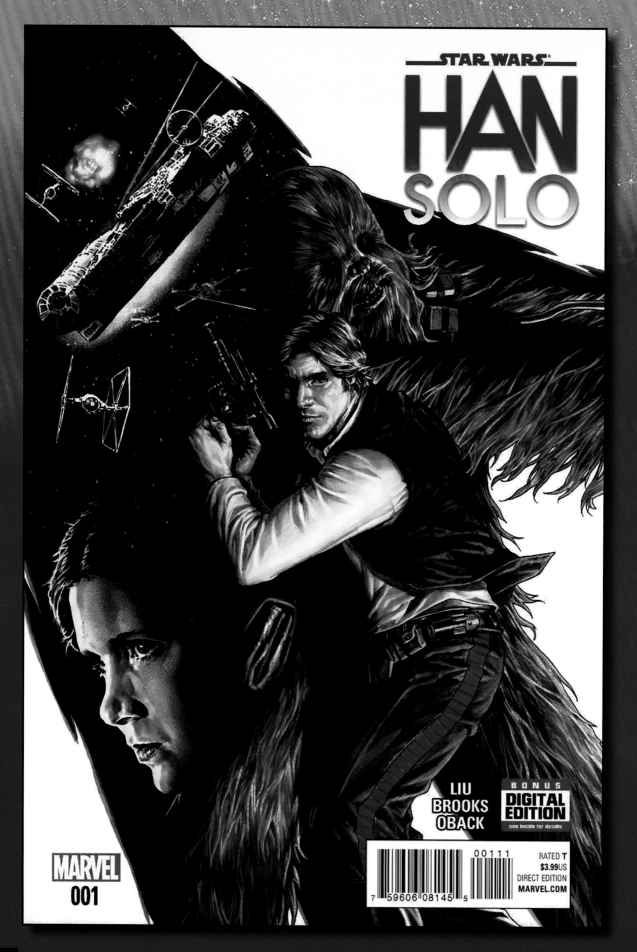

> ## "MY FAVORITE THING ABOUT HAN IS THAT HE IS A SCREW-UP."

as a hero and a rebel. He's always dreamed of entering this race, but now that he's in it, he's on a secret rebel mission! He has to choose between his new friends and the chance for fortune and glory. Wait, wrong movie... But it still fits!

What makes Han so appealing?
My favorite thing about Han is that he is a screw-up. He isn't a typical hero because he spends half of his time messing up, and the other half trying to clean up those messes. You root for him to make good because he's so charming and likeable while doing it. He usually does, but that doesn't change the fact that he gets himself into problems in the first place.

How does Chewie fit into the story? If the Wookiee wins, will he get a medal?
First off, we confirmed in the *Chewbacca* miniseries that Chewie did get a medal after the Battle of Yavin—he just doesn't wear it for cultural reasons to do with his bandolier. As for the Dragon Void Run, I am not so sure they give medals to the winner. We'll have to see when we hit the finish line —if we hit the finish line!

Han Solo #1 has some beautiful variant covers. How do you attract so many great artists?
We're incredibly lucky in that Marvel has access to the best artists in the comic-book business, and so many of them share our deep love of *Star Wars*. Everyone wants to show their take on Luke and Darth Vader; their take on Rey and Kylo Ren; and their

take on Han Solo. It's an embarrassment of riches in that respect. We're happy to be able to share so many visions of this universe with the readers.

What's a standard day in the life of a *Star Wars* comics editor?
Every day is a mad world of plate-spinning. I work on several issues at once, so I have pages of art coming in from various pencilers, inkers, and colorists. I review each one and send back any notes I have, which sometimes just means telling the artists how terrific it all looks. There are also scripts from writers that I need to read and comment on; lettering drafts I need to give notes on; and final proofs of comic-books being printed that week, which I need to check and sign off. On top of all that, there are planning meetings and calls with Lucasfilm to discuss new and ongoing projects. My wife plays games on her cellphone where you run a virtual cake shop or whatever: taking orders, baking cakes, delivering them, and then buying more ovens and ingredients. I can't play those games—that's my life every day, but with less frosting.

In a previous *Insider* interview, you've hinted at a Jar Jar Binks miniseries. We can't let you go without asking for an update on that!
Right now, I've decided to hold off on the Jar Jar story until I get George Lucas' blessing. But for some reason he won't take my calls... ☻

This page: Variant cover art by artist Scott Koblish. Opposite page: Newsstand cover art by Lee Bermejo.

> ### MORE TO SAY
>
> Follow Jordan D. White on Twitter @cracksh0t
> Follow Michael Kogge online at michaelkogge.com or on Twitter @michaelkogge
>
> ### HAVE YOU?

STAR WARS COMICS

APHRA
TAKES FLIGHT

MARVEL'S ANARCHIC ARCHAEOLOGIST IS CAUSING CHAOS ACROSS THE *STAR WARS* GALAXY. MEGAN CROUSE MET THE TEAM BEHIND *DOCTOR APHRA*.

MEET TEAM APHRA
KIERON GILLEN, *WRITER*
KEV WALKER, *ARTIST*
HEATHER ANTOS, *ASSISTANT EDITOR, MARVEL*
JORDAN D. WHITE, *EDITOR, MARVEL*
FRANK PARISI, *SENIOR EDITOR, LUCASFILM*

The groundbreaking run of Marvel Comics' *Darth Vader* introduced rogue archaeologist Doctor Aphra into *Star Wars* lore. An instant hit with readers, she now stars in her own comic book series.

This is the first Marvel *Star Wars* series led by a character created for the comics. What drew you to Aphra's story?

Heather Antos: What's not interesting when it comes to Aphra? She's such a fascinating character—she's not a hero, but she isn't a villain either. It's a terribly fun mindset to play with, this moral gray area. Not to mention she has some of the best sidekicks the *Star Wars* universe has ever seen! Between working for the galaxy's most evil Sith Lord, and then turning hero to help Princess Leia fight her way out of a hostage situation, you never know what sort of trouble Aphra will get herself into—and out of! Every page is an adventure.

Frank Parisi: The draw was Aphra herself. Aphra is a revolutionary, and I don't use that term with any thought of politics or ideology. It's clear that life hasn't treated Aphra fairly... which isn't life's job, I suppose. She's been on the receiving end of some tough, tough times and has dealt with some tough, tough people. But she's the kind of person who [spoiler alert!] gets lobbed out of an airlock by Darth Vader into

the frigid emptiness of space, brushes herself off, and says to her crew with a grin, "That sucked. Now let's get back to work!" While I wouldn't go so far as to call her optimistic, she is most definitely anti-pessimistic and goal-driven, and to retain that attitude and sense of humor while contending against the worst life the galaxy has to throw at you… it's a revolutionary act. It certainly does not hurt that Kieron Gillen is a storytelling dynamo to boot.

Jordan D. White: I agree with Heather and Frank—Aphra herself was just a joy in every issue of Darth Vader. We could not resist. When Kieron told us he had thought of a way to save her from Vader's vengeance, we all rejoiced! If she can be a complete delight in the midst of the bleakness of the Darth Vader series, how much more fun could we have on her own adventures? That said, I think I might disagree that she isn't a villain. She's out for herself above

all, and it's certainly not her most admirable trait. If *Darth Vader* was our *Breaking Bad*, then *Doctor Aphra* is our *Better Call Saul*. You might love how charming she is, you might be rooting for her at every turn… but she's probably not going to do the "right" thing. But that's why she's relatable.

Kieron Gillen, you brought Aphra to life in the *Darth Vader* series. What was it like to learn that Aphra would have her own story?
Kieron Gillen: It was great. That she'd made enough of an impression to get her own series is amazing. I have never had a character I created go on to have their own book. For Aphra to be my first, and the first non-movie *Star Wars* character to have an ongoing series of her own, is obviously pretty humbling.

What was it about Aphra that made her a good fit for an ongoing series?
KG: In a real way, the series itself is

the answer to this question—but I'd pick a few key ones. She's a big, iconic, archetypal character who fits into *Star Wars* as a concept, but hasn't been done before… but also she's a big, iconic, archetypal character with a hard twist. She's very much a two-fisted archaeologist adventurer. She goes and digs up the past, and punches people along the way. That's a very clean story engine for a character. Then there's the other side—that she's immoral. The book runs on the odd tension of having someone who is often likable, and even occasionally relatable… but you can't be sure where her ethical line is. "What will she do? What won't she do?" That's unusual, and adds a certain tension.

A second reason—and the main reason why I took the job—was that as much fun as she had in *Darth Vader*, there were huge chunks of her we hadn't explored. She's an archaeologist, but I wanted to excavate her personality.

Oh—and with *Star Wars'* long history, her being an archaeologist obviously lets us introduce a bunch of fun stuff. Who doesn't like knowing more about the history of the *Star Wars* universe?

Do you have a lot of back-and-forth conversations in regards to the art and the script? What's your collaboration process?
KG: Kev is fantastic. He's the sort of artist who annotates his thumbnails and talks about his choices. I consider my scripts the start of a conversation rather than a diktat. Kevin certainly rolls with that—he's a fantastic visual storyteller and writer, and that comes across in his active engagement with the stories, especially when world-building. There are visual elements Kevin adds that I then work back into my thinking—like stuff in his design for Captain Tolvan, the first arc's main antagonist. It's been wonderful.

> "SHE'S VERY MUCH A TWO-FISTED ARCHAEOLOGIST ADVENTURER. SHE GOES AND DIGS UP THE PAST, AND PUNCHES PEOPLE ALONG THE WAY. THAT'S A VERY CLEAN STORY ENGINE FOR A CHARACTER"

Kev Walker: I always worry that I might come across as a bit of a thug when it comes to my writers. I have a habit of scribbling all over their carefully crafted prose without a second thought. Ideas are cruel. They just hit you round the head without any regard for the creative process.

I've found that honesty is the best policy—I draw it the way I think it should look, regardless of the script, but always with the caveat that these are just ideas and anyone else has exactly the same right to scribble all over my layouts and notes. The writer, the editors, or Lucasfilm always make me qualify an idea, and if it strays too far from the path, they gently poke me with a stick until I draw what they're happy with.

Seriously, though, I've been blessed with writers and editors tell if she would survive or not.

Now that she has her own book, things change. She's funny, but she's not the comic relief anymore—she plays the lead and gets to do the heavy lifting. With Vader offstage, everyone else appears more threatening in his absence. Doctor Aphra is a fun and often sarcastic presence, but she's also a darker creature.

What inspired the character of Aphra's father?

KG: We explored a little of her background in *Darth Vader* when we revealed Aphra's mother was killed by raiders during the war, after splitting with her father. Pretty much the first thing I knew when I started thinking about Aphra as an ongoing character is we would have to meet the father as soon as possible. If we're going to talk cynic, who believes he never cared for anything but his obsession. Gradually they realize they both have each other wrong, and trying to get that across, as both people change, is a challenge I relish.

We see some of Aphra's school days in the comics too. Were those scenes you had in mind for a long time and are only showing now, or was developing Aphra's history part of the process of making the new series?

KG: The core is there, but there is room to develop her history. Thanoth hinted that Aphra's doctorate had a question mark over it in the *Darth Vader* series, so there was certainly foreshadowing. That she manipulated an ethically questionable superior was always there. Of course, Aphra cheated. Aphra could have earned it by

> "THE WRITER, THE EDITORS, OR LUCASFILM WILL ALWAYS MAKE ME QUALIFY AN IDEA, AND IF IT STRAYS TOO FAR FROM THE PATH, THEY GENTLY POKE ME WITH A STICK UNTIL I DRAW WHAT THEY'RE HAPPY WITH."

who don't consider a book done until the print deadline hit. It's an evolutionary process, and everyone pitches in to try and make this book the best that we can in the time we have; pushing and pulling the thing into shape.

Kieron, you developed Aphra as a foil to Darth Vader. What's it like having her lead her own story?

KG: It changes things a bit. In *Darth Vader*, she existed to do the things that Vader couldn't do. Most of all, talk. Vader has to be stoic and laconic. The more words he says, the more it becomes untrue to the character. Vader needed someone at his side to do all that quiet exposition; making her nervously talkative is a fun contrast to the Dark Lord himself. Equally, there's the comedy she added. Plus, there is a bit of tension—we knew that Vader wouldn't die, but we couldn't about Aphra's past, he's essential. This is a book about emotional archaeology as well as actual archaeology, if you see what I mean. He is like Aphra in many ways, but desperately, incredibly unlike her in others.

KW: When I first drew him, I didn't really have much of an idea of his background. It would be easy to draw parallels with Indiana Jones and his father. To be honest, Aphra's father is way more closeted, idealistic, and naïve than Henry Jones ever was. When we first meet Aphra's father, he's literally in an ivory tower: he's an academic with no concept of what's going on in the world around him, let alone the galaxy at large. He's let all sorts of important things fall by the wayside, in pursuit of a myth. Aphra begins this story as his polar opposite, a complete egotist and herself, but she'd much prefer to cheat. Cheating is what smart people do in her world.

Triple Zero and Bee Tee are both friends and threats. What can you tell us about how they'll help out Aphra?

KG: They're our Greek chorus in many ways, pointing out the ironies and hypocrisies in the cast in their own monstrous idiom. But, like Aphra, they become a little darker in the absence of Vader. Yes, they're funny, but in the first episode they're already murdering people by themselves, for their own ends. You have to suspect they're a ticking time bomb. As Triple Zero said back in *Darth Vader*, "Heaven help everyone if I get bored."

What is your favorite moment featuring the droids?

KG: There are too many to pick ▶

143

from. The first one which I genuinely loved from way back in issue four of *Darth Vader* was when he said, "Hahahaha! You're on fire and also dead!" The one which tickles me in *Doctor Aphra* is from the second issue, where Triple Zero is threatening to torture Aphra's father. "Your daughter is a truly horrible person. You must be very proud." Which is funny, not least because of how Kev drew the astounding array of torture implements from his hand, but because it also serves as a good character beat for Aphra. I said that they're the Greek chorus? Well, that's an example. Aphra's smart enough to know that if that droid is very much pro-you that something has gone horribly, horribly wrong.

KW: There's a gag in *Doctor Aphra* issue five which, for obvious reasons, I can't tell you about (I haven't even finished drawing it yet), but it continually makes me chuckle. Actually I have to stop myself from running too far with the humor, because this is *Star Wars*, not *SpongeBob SquarePants*. I mean, I thought I was pushing it a little with Triple Zero's torture hands in issue two. How could he possibly have a circular saw and a blowtorch in his hands? They wouldn't fit. But it is funny. Like Beetee suddenly having bazookas and grenade launchers. It's cartoon humor, but sometimes if you get it just right, it makes things scarier, like getting well-loved comic actors to play serial killers in movies or TV. The spoonful of sugar laced with poison.

Then there's Black Krrsantan, who is a bit of an anti-Chewbacca. What can you tell us about his role?
KG: One of my favorite things about *Doctor Aphra* is that we get a chance to really dig into Krrsantan. He gets some of the best action beats in the whole series, and his past comes into play

APHRA'S CREW

TRIPLE ZERO
A protocol droid, specializing in etiquette, customs, translation, and torture. Once designated to serve Darth Vader, wherever Triple Zero and his counterpart Bee Tee One go, carnage will follow.

BEE TEE ONE
Cunningly disguised as a astromech droid Bee Tee One is an assassin droid (a blastomech). Armed and dangerous, Bee Tee One was created by the Galactic Empire's Tarkin Initiative.

BLACK KRRSANTAN
A Wookiee bounty hunter also known as Santy, Black Krrsantan is deemed by Boba Fett to be one of the best in his field. Krrsantan was scarred in a skirmish with Obi-Wan Kenobi.

in a big way. Even from the start, the relationship with Aphra lets us show a lot about the book. He hangs with Aphra, sure, but only because she owes him a lot of money and he considers her an investment… and she has promised to locate the people who trained him to be a gladiator. Not that he minded being a gladiator, he just objects to anyone making him do anything.

KW: I like drawing Wookiees. That's all. I just wanted to say that.

Kev, did you have a favorite character design in the new series?
KW: I do: Tolvan. I can't say why, because it'd be a spoiler, and it's not just because I got to design her, but because I (sort of) know what's going to happen to her, which influences how I draw her. Actually, I enjoy drawing all the characters, and if there's something about their design I don't like, I find some way I can change it. Because these are characters who get dirty, get injured, have stuff that tears or breaks, or is unsuitable for the environment they are in, I get to continually mix things up—it helps to keep things fresh.

What was the thought process behind Aphra's costume?
KW: Well it's just trying to make things fit with the *Star Wars* universe. So the long duster coats in issues two and three came

about from looking at the outfits the rebels wore on Endor in *Return of the Jedi.* They have a reason for wearing the things they do, and it's not just to look cool. I'm making things up, but everything still needs to feel part of a whole and to echo things that have been seen in the *Star Wars* universe. The Academic installation harkens back to Bespin Cloud City on purpose, and not just because it might have been built by the same company, but because it grounds the location and makes it a part of the things we have seen on-screen. Soo-Tath the money-lender in issue one has a hat based on a Ralph McQuarrie concept for Bib Fortuna that never got used.

If you could see Doctor Aphra interact with any *Star Wars* character she hasn't met before, who would it be?
KG: I can just see an older Aphra throwing her arm around Kylo Ren and saying "Oh, the things I could tell you about your Grandpops."

KW: Jar Jar Binks! It would make a lot of people happy. Do you realize that without him bumping into Qui-Gon and Obi-Wan on Naboo, nothing else would have happened the way it has? It could all have been so different. Makes you think... ☻

< The crew of the *Ark Angel* confront a figure from the doctor's past in *Doctor Aphra* #2. Art by Kev Walker.

145

MY STAR WARS

SUAVE, COOL, AND CHARMING, BILLY DEE WILLIAMS (THE "DEE" PART STANDS FOR "DECEMBER") IS MUCH LIKE HIS ON-SCREEN COUNTERPART, LANDO CALRISSIAN. *INSIDER* MET THE MAN HIMSELF TO DISCUSS ART, BETRAYAL, AND BUFFING UP! INTERVIEW BY MARK NEWBOLD & JAMES BURNS

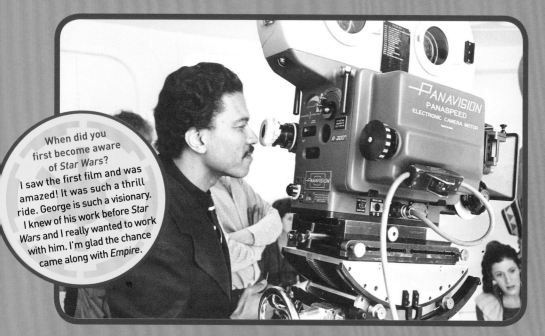

When did you first become aware of *Star Wars*?
I saw the first film and was amazed! It was such a thrill ride. George is such a visionary. I knew of his work before *Star Wars* and I really wanted to work with him. I'm glad the chance came along with *Empire*.

Where is the strangest place you've been recognized?
I get approached almost everywhere I go. I am very pleased to meet fans, and I will always put down my dinner fork to say hi. Without the fans, I would not be where I am today. That is why I like going to conventions: I get to give back to the fans.

Can you reveal something about yourself that will surprise your fans?
Some people have no idea that I was an artist before I was an actor. My art is very important to me.

Do you have a favorite scene?
I loved going up against Darth Vader in *Empire*. It might have only been for a second, but I did stand up to him!

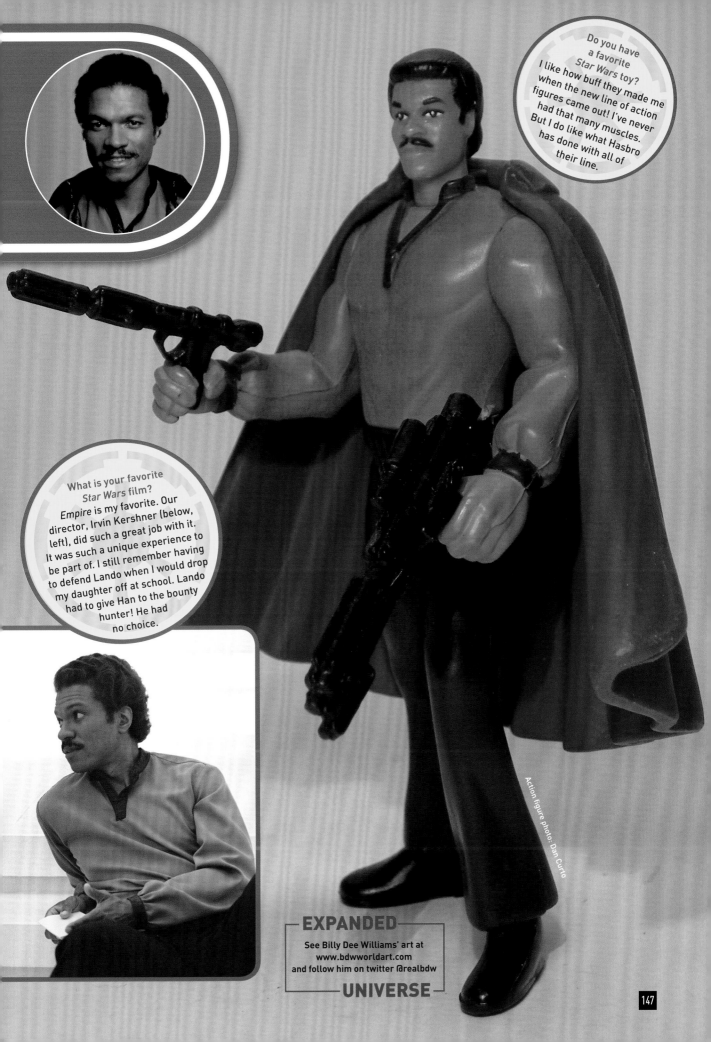

Do you have a favorite *Star Wars* toy?
I like how buff they made me when the new line of action figures came out! I've never had that many muscles. But I do like what Hasbro has done with all of their line.

What is your favorite *Star Wars* film?
Empire is my favorite. Our director, Irvin Kershner (below, left), did such a great job with it. It was such a unique experience to be part of. I still remember having to defend Lando when I would drop my daughter off at school. Lando had to give Han to the bounty hunter! He had no choice.

Action figure photo: Dan Curto

147

Capes Maketh The Calrissian

A galaxy of costumes from *Solo: A Star Wars Story*

Headed by David Crossman and Glyn Dillon, the team assembled for *Solo*'s costume department designed and handmade more than 1,000 outfits for the movie's rogues and scoundrels, including the gang that made the Kessel Run. *Insider* reveals the thought processes behind the threads for the blockbuster's key characters.

WORDS: CHRISTOPHER COOPER

F or David Crossman, costume supervisor on *Star Wars: The Force Awakens* (2015) and *The Last Jedi* (2017), the chance to co-design the costumes for *Solo: A Star Wars Story* (2018) was a dream come true. "Han Solo is my favorite character from the original trilogy films," he says. "Han is the epitome of cool, and his is such an iconic look for a designer to explore."

Glyn Dillon, who also shared costume designer reponsibilities with Crossman on *Rogue One: A Star Wars Story* (2016) adds, "The characters that Han meets throughout his journey are also so layered and so rich. They presented fantastic opportunities for us."

The costume team crafted an incredible wardrobe of clothes for the principal cast, alien creatures, and the vast number of crowd players who add color to every shot.

Intent on remaining faithful to the aesthetics of *A New Hope* (1977), Crossman and Dillon took inspiration from a myriad of 1970s references and movies, including gritty revisionist Westerns such as Robert Altman's *McCabe & Mrs. Miller* (1971). The majority of the costumes were designed and produced in-house, from wide-brimmed hats and fringed jackets to the bright indigenous clothing of Savareen's nomadic tribes, and the high-fashion gear worn by the guests of Dryden Vos.

With such a wide variety of looks required for the different worlds of *Solo*, what does Crossman think it is that makes a *Star Wars* costume fit for that universe? "It's something real," he suggests, "something that audiences recognize and can relate to from their own lives, that's taken from history and mixed with fantasy elements. That's what gives a costume the *Star Wars* feel."

> "We liked the idea that the look becomes Han Solo during the course of the film, as he acquires pieces from Beckett and other characters."
> **David Crossman**

Han Solo

→ "Han Solo's look is so classic, so iconic, that we didn't want to veer too far away from the original costume," reveals Crossman, "but we wanted to see how he got there. We liked the idea that the look becomes Han Solo during the course of the film, as he acquires pieces from Beckett and other characters. The more people he meets, the more he gathers and establishes his own identity."

The designers had several looks to create for Han (Alden Ehrenreich) on his costume journey, starting with his Corellian scrumrat gear. Says Dillon, "We were looking at rock bands like The Clash for inspiration, and we arrived at a 1980s punk look mixed with a 1950s element."

The costume consists of a leather vest—painted white to indicate he "belongs" to the White Worms—customized with trinkets he's picked up along the way. "It works as a negative of the classic costume," Dillon explains. "The vest is white, the shirt is dark, and the Corellian blood stripe on his pants is faintly visible. He's identifiable as Han Solo, but the costume suggests youth and rebellion."

As Crossman and Dillon imply, Han Solo's look evolves gradually throughout the movie. He ditches his mudtrooper uniform but keeps the boots, for example. "The boots become Han's, which he carries on through his journey," confirms Grossman. From Beckett he gets his gun belt, DL-44 blaster, and his jacket. "By the time he's reunited with Qi'ra on Dryden's Yacht, he is starting to look almost like the Han Solo that everyone knows," Crossman notes.

Han's Steve McQueen-styled suede jacket directly harks back to design cues from the 1977 original, as Crossman explains: "There was a lovely 1960s jacket we saw somewhere in London on which we based the suede jacket. Everything in Han Solo's *A New Hope* look is very cropped so we aimed for that, keeping the sleeves shorter, and the jacket length short so he can reach his blaster."

01 Concept art by Glyn Dillon.

02

"**In one of the first drawings of Lando that we did, we drew him with a yellow shirt, and that was it. That was Lando!**"

Glyn Dillon

03

04

ᒐᛘᐯ ᔕᛕᑌᐯᒐ ᔕ᠘ᑌᐯᛕᔕᐯᒐ

Lando Calrissian

→ The designers again turned to musical influences for Lando's costumes, specifically the flamboyance of Jimi Hendrix, Prince, and Marvin Gaye. Used to rendering countless concepts before landing on a look that satisfies the needs of the script, with Donald Glover's Lando the process turned out to be easier than expected.

"Lando is such a colorful character, we wanted to have some fun with his costumes by bringing in some vibrancy and very strong colors," says Dillon. "In one of the first drawings of Lando that we did, we drew him with a yellow shirt, and that was it. That was Lando!"

Lando's extensive cape collection, seen hanging in his walk-in closet on the *Millennium Falcon*, presented a great opportunity for the designers to expand his wardrobe beyond anything Lando would have time to actually wear in the movie. In all, 30 capes were created for the closet.

"Audiences don't see Lando in much else than his yellow shirt," says Crossman, "so we tried to incorporate every texture into the closet, mixing patterns, velvets, and leathers, in order to get as great a variety on screen as we feasibly could."

For the final sequence in the movie, where Han and Chewie finally gain posession of the *Falcon* after a card game in a tropical environment, the designers fashioned a Hawaiian-styled shirt for Lando. A sketch of an air speeder by Ralph McQuarrie sparked the inspiration for the pattern on the shirt.

02 Concept art by Glyn Dillon.

03 Concept art by Glyn Dillon.

04 Concept art by David Crossman.

‎ᔑ ‎ᒲᔑ‎ᑑᔑ‎ᒲᔑ
‎ᒲᔑ‎ᑑᔑ‎ᒲᔑ

Tobias Beckett

→ "We wanted to give Beckett the feeling of a mentor for Han," Dillon says of the costume they designed for Tobias Beckett (Woody Harrelson). The character's long, pale duster coat, worn over a dark flight suit, was intended to engender a feeling of familiarity and therefore of trust. "Beckett wears the costume almost throughout the entire movie," says Crossman. "Sometimes that's helpful for certain characters. People identify with them better."

His one major costume change sees Beckett wearing Lando's armor from *Return of the Jedi* (1983) as a disguise during the Kessel action sequences. "The helmet was actually based on a baseball glove," says Dillon. "It was great fun recreating that costume. It's one of those references that *Star Wars* fans will love—that maybe Beckett left it on the *Falcon*, and years later Lando digs it out when he needs a disguise to rescue Han from Jabba."

05

> ## "We wanted to give Beckett the feeling of a mentor for Han."
> **Glyn Dillon**

05 Concept art by Adam Brockbank.

06 Concept art by Glyn Dillon.

07 Concept art by Glyn Dillon.

06

07

‎ᒲᔑ ‎ᑑᔑ
‎ᒲᔑ‎ᑑᔑ ‎ᑑᔑ

Val

→ "Val was a fun one to do," says Dillon. "She's strong and she's cool, so we went with leather and a backward apron skirt that is quite punky but also very *Star Wars*."

Thandie Newton, who plays Val, collaborated closely with the designers on her costumes. "Different actors have different ways into their characters," says Newton. "For me, the costume and the whole look of the character is when I finally feel the person I'm playing, and Val's costume was such a fantastic evolution. I have two costumes, both very functional, but the second one had so many gadgets over it, and every element had a function. It felt like I had a layer of robotic strength, and that the costume told a story."

‎ᑑᔑ‎ᑑᔑ
‎ᒲᔑ‎ᑑᔑ‎ᑑᔑ

Dryden Vos

→ Making the most of Paul Bettany's imposing presence, the designers dressed the Dryden Vos actor in darkly beautiful tailored fabrics. To further accentuate the character's sense of cool menace, they crafted a cape that appears to have grown onto the jacket, becoming integral to it and lending Vos a formidable silhouette.

"There has to be a connection between Dryden and Qi'ra that presents itself as a clear threat to Han, not just a physical threat but also a romantic one," says Dillon of the contrast between Solo and Vos. "This was something we felt was important to express in Dryden's costume, that he look charming, suave, but dangerous too."

"Her look needed to be sophisticated, so we went with a Lauren Bacall-inspired beautiful black silk dress."
David Crossman

Qi'ra

→ Qi'ra (played by Emilia Clarke) presented numerous opportunities to the designers to chart the character's growth, as she moves from street kid to glamorous gang lynchpin over the course of the movie. Her costumes become more practical as the narrative dictates, but always retain a sophisticated edge. Qi'ra's Corellian costume may share punkish 80s influences with Han's scrumrat outfit, but her oversized boyfriend jacket, leather skirt, and pointy boots fizz with style. Influences from the Western genre, combined with those of a film noir femme fatale, are very clear in both her Fort Ypso saloon and *First Light* outfits.

"We wanted to create a look that blows Han away when he sees her again," relates Dillon. "She has to be recognizable, but there has to be something in the way she dresses that gives her that ambiguous edge: is she dangerous, can he trust her?"

"She's second-in-command of this criminal gang," Crossman adds. "Her look needed to be sophisticated, so we went with a Lauren Bacall-inspired beautiful black silk dress. We gave it powerful shoulders, and shiny black jewelry that incorporates the Crimson Dawn logo."

08

09

08 Concept art by Adam Brockbank.

09 Concept art by Glyn Dillon.

Lando's Pride And Joy

WE MAY BE MORE USED TO SEEING THE *MILLENNIUM FALCON* LOOKING ROUGH AROUND THE EDGES, BUT AS *SOLO: A STAR WARS STORY* REVEALS, THE FASTEST HUNK OF JUNK IN THE GALAXY ONCE HAD THE LOOKS TO MATCH.

WORDS: CHRISTOPHER COOPER

T he *Millennium Falcon* is the apple of Lando Calrissian's eye. A heavily modified Corellian Engineering Corporation YT-1300 light freighter, the *Falcon* was already a much-travelled ship when it became the property of Calrissian, and the vessel has been extensively refitted to meet his discerning tastes. Docked within the arms of the *Falcon*'s forward mandibles sits a detachable escape craft, lending to the ship's sleek and distinctive profile, while the minimalist white, black, and yellow interior reflects the gambler's appreciation for sharp lines and expensive finishes.

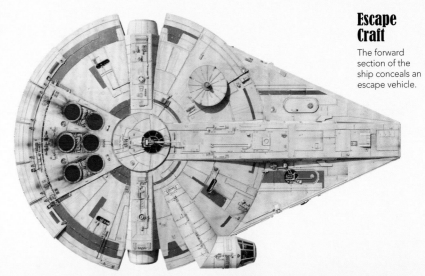

Escape Craft

The forward section of the ship conceals an escape vehicle.

Lando Calrissian (Donald Glover) at the controls of his ship.

Chewbacca (Joonas Suotamo) and Han Solo (Alden Ehrenreich) make themselves at home.

The view from the *Falcon*'s cockpit.

The Cockpit

Dominated by its large transparisteel viewport, the *Millennium Falcon*'s cockpit is as clean and high-spec as the rest of the ship, and can seat the pilot, co-pilot, and two additional crew members.

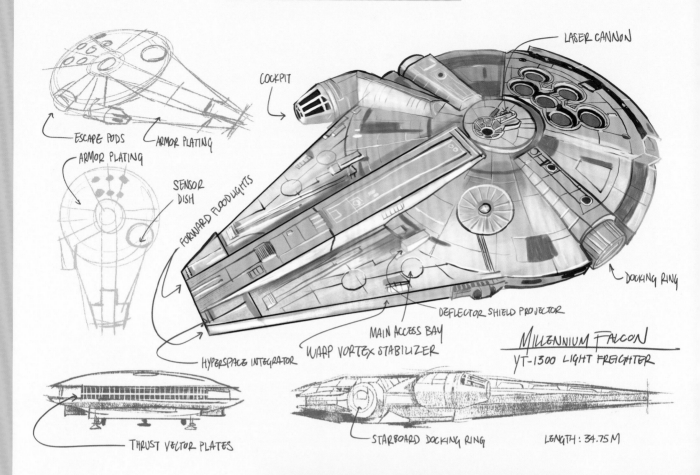

LASER CANNON

COCKPIT

ESCAPE PODS

ARMOR PLATING

ARMOR PLATING

SENSOR DISH

FORWARD FLOODLIGHTS

DOCKING RING

DEFLECTOR SHIELD PROJECTOR

MAIN ACCESS BAY

WARP VORTEX STABILIZER

HYPERSPACE INTEGRATOR

MILLENNIUM FALCON
YT-1300 LIGHT FREIGHTER

THRUST VECTOR PLATES

STARBOARD DOCKING RING

LENGTH: 34.75 M

Main Hold

Calrissian has converted the main hold into an area he uses primarily for entertaining invited guests or for relaxing between gaming engagements. A large recliner dominates the space, disguising an unsightly maintenance panel beneath.

Han and Beckett (Woody Harrelson) join Chewie at the holochess table.

Chewbacca contemplates a solo game of dejarik.

Holochess Table

Taking pride of place in the *Falcon*'s main hold is Calrissian's holochess table, where he enjoys the odd game of dejarik and practices his card skills.

Smuggling Compartments

Before becoming a professional gambler, Lando Calrissian's previous career as a space smuggler required the use of secret compartments aboard his ship to store contraband. Some of these were hidden beneath the decking of the main corridor, which runs around the center of the ship.

Qi'ra (Emilia Clarke) tries one of Lando's capes on for size.

Lando's Wardrobe

A man of impeccable taste and style, Calrissian maintains a fashionable wardrobe aboard his ship to enhance his image as a successful sportsman.

The main hold includes a technical station (far right).

A view into the main hold from the forward corridor.

Han Solo (Alden Ehrenreich) explores the *Falcon*.

Technical Station

On a bulkhead opposite the main hold's holochess table, a technical station installed by a previous owner allows Calrissian and his co-pilot, the self-built droid L3-37, to monitor the ship's operational status.

JONATHAN KASDAN

WRITING *SOLO: A STAR WARS STORY*

When Jonathan Kasdan was born, a mere nine months before *Star Wars: The Empire Strikes Back* opened in June of 1980, his father—screenwriter Lawrence Kasdan—was already knee-deep in the storytelling and screenwriting of the *Star Wars* films. With such an auspicious connection to the *Star Wars* mythology, we can only assume that the Force must have had some influence on tiny Jon. Why? Because he grew up to eventually co-write *Solo: A Star Wars Story* (2018) with his father, and that's the epitome of full-circle destiny.

Star Wars Insider recently had the chance to talk with Jon about crafting our favorite scoundrel's origin tale, and what it has meant for him to be a part of the universe that so significantly helped shape his creative path.

WORDS: TARA BENNETT

01

01 Beckett's
team arrive
on Kessel.

02 Father
and son
writing team,
Lawrence
(right) and
Jon Kasdan.
(Opposite
page)

03 Besties Han
and Chewie.
(Opposite
page)

04 Alden
Ehrenreich as
Han Solo in
Solo: A Star
Wars Story.
(Opposite
page)

Star Wars Insider: Let's start from the beginning. Was there a specific historical beat in Han's backstory that rooted the screenplay, or that created a foundation for the story?
Before I got involved, when my dad was preparing for *Star Wars: The Force Awakens* (2015), he wanted to do this as his one and only last *Star Wars* thing. He was really interested in the years that would be formative to Han's identity—which he considered to be the end of his adolescence and the beginning of his young manhood. He wanted to get a taste of his childhood and see what that was like, but he really wanted the bulk of the story to be about Han finding, essentially, his identity and his career in this criminal underworld; becoming a smuggler and meeting Chewbacca. He felt like those events were entwined. And so that was part of the premise going in as we started working together.

When you're looking at this period in Han's life, there's a threshold of maturity in terms of how far to take him. Did you play with that?
We did. And again, some of these were decisions that Larry had made, I think, not even consciously. What he imagined when the idea popped into his head, or when it was suggested that there'd be a young Han Solo movie, was that he didn't want to place it right up to where we meet Han in Mos Eisley. Larry thought the transition that made the character into 'that guy' was a long and complex one. He wanted to follow certain events in his life. He arrived [at the premise] that we could talk about a younger version of the character and aim it toward the Han that we all recognize, but not have him be there by the end of the movie. And that's a tricky thing because there's a certain expectation. Some people say, "Well, why isn't he more like the guy at Mos Eisley [in *Star Wars: A New Hope (1977)*]?" And other people say, "Well, he's too much like the guy at Mos Eisley." And you sort of get both. The tricky thing about writing a character like Han is that he's personal to so many people.

I think you see it in the difference of taking on someone like [Marvel's] Black Panther, for example. We know who he is, and we know he looks super cool and that he's a black super hero, but we don't have an opinion about his life the way we do with Han Solo. So, one of the fundamental challenges of writing this story was how much to give, and how to stoke those fires and dance with people's expectations a little.

Was there anything that you ended up changing Larry's mind about, or had him see in a different way?
The idea that Han would actually be with the Empire in the beginning of the story was something that evolved. Initially, that wasn't

> "WE DID WANT TO GIVE IT THIS FEELING OF A GALAXY IN CHAOS. VERY EARLY ON, WE HIT ON THE NOTION THAT IT WAS AKIN TO THE WILD WEST."

02

03

04

"WE WANTED EVERYONE IN THE MOVIE TO HAVE A MORE NUANCED, MORE COMPLICATED, AND MORALLY AMBIGUOUS SET OF GOALS AND DESIRES THAN IN ANY OTHER *STAR WARS* MOVIE TO DATE."

exactly the concept, but as we started to explore the moment in history that this was taking place, [we realized] it was a complicated one in the *Star Wars* galaxy. We did want to give it this feeling of a galaxy in chaos. Very early on, we hit on the notion that it was akin to the Wild West, where there was a sense of conquering powers that worked, but also a lot of law-breaking and opportunity for people to make money, and be violent and so forth.

Beckett was an original character that you brought into the world. There's a beautiful swagger to Woody Harrelson's performance that you can see in future Han—was Beckett always crafted as a mentor/adversary for Han?
Absolutely. Before I became involved, there were elements that Larry was interested in and knew he wanted to touch on, but there was no story. At the point when I got involved, we both read *Treasure Island* as a maturation story. It's about a guy who goes from a more innocent existence, and through immediate people who are complicated, develops a little bit of experience of the world. We wanted to give Han a character that was as rich and fun as Long John Silver, who could really influence who he becomes. So, we definitely wanted to do exactly that, and create a sort of pre-Han Han. Then at the end of the story, we gave that character, Beckett, a very similar predicament to the one that Han faced in *A New Hope,* where he left Luke and the Rebellion behind. But here we had Beckett actually opt out, and rather than rescue his friend, he betrayed him. We thought that could highlight the nature of Han. Beckett is his role model, but in his heart, Han couldn't do likewise when the same opportunities were presented to him. Han's undoing, and his greatest strength, has always been that he's got a lot of love in him.

You presented a bit of Chewie's backstory, revealing that he has a story arc where he chooses to stay with Han. Was there even more to that arc?
There's a lot more. There were other Wookiee characters that briefly appeared in the story, in addition to Sagwa, who Chewbacca helps on ►

05

Kessel. We wanted to get a sense—which I think is indicated pretty clearly in the first few movies and a little less clearly in the prequels—that this has a parallel to the broken nations of Native American culture. It's the idea of individuals whose people have been destroyed and are trying to make their way in a world where their culture has basically been ravaged by Imperial power. So, we always wanted to give it a little flavor of that. We stumbled on the idea of Chewie telling his story at the campfire, and we felt like there was something really rich in how he got into that situation, and how he was very much like Han: alone in the universe, in search of something, someone, or some people that may, or may not, even be alive. We thought that would reinforce the theme—which has always been there, through all of the *Star Wars* movies—of people making their own families.

We've always perceived Han as being framed around the singular romantic relationship he has with Leia, which was built during the original trilogy. But you got to create the woman who would influence all future romances in his life. Who did you need Qi'ra to be? We wanted everyone in the movie to have a more nuanced, more complicated, and morally ambiguous set of goals and desires than in any

> **"QI'RA ABANDONING HAN WOULD BECOME A REALLY SEMINAL MOMENT IN HIS LIFE, WHERE HE WOULD LEARN THAT THERE WERE THINGS MORE COMPLICATED THAN HIS YOUTHFUL, ROMANTIC IMPULSES."**

06

07

JONATHAN KASDAN: ON-SCREEN AND OFF

Born September 30, 1979, talented actor, writer, and director Jon Kasdan may be best known to *Star Wars* fans as one half of the father-son writing duo behind *Solo: A Star Wars Story* (2018), but the road to the galaxy far, far away has, in fact, been a long and varied one—and not always easy.

Born to Lawrence and Meg Kasdan (both successful writers and directors), Jon made his acting debut when he was just four years old in *The Big Chill* (1983)—a film penned by his father. A role in the acclaimed Western *Silverado* (1985) soon followed, with smaller parts in *The Accidental Tourist* (1988), *I Love You to Death* (1990), *Wyatt Earp* (1994), *Slackers* (2002), *Big Trouble* (2002), *Dreamcatcher* (2003) and *Darling Companion* (2012) continuing his big-screen journey. Appearances in *Freaks and Geeks* (1999), and *Dawson's Creek* (2002) also ensured he became a familiar face on TV.

However, having been diagnosed with Hodgkin's Lymphoma at just 17 years old, the younger Kasdan faced a difficult battle to successfully overcome the disease—which he ultimately did with the love and support of his family. He continued to carve out a career for himself as an actor, before seguing into a different role.

As with both his father and brother (Jake), Jon ultimately turned his attention to a career on the other side of the camera, and in 2007, after amassing writing credits on TV shows *Freaks and Geeks* and *Dawson's Creek*, made his directorial debut with the Kristen Stewart romantic comedy *In the Land of Women*, followed by the Sundance Film Festival award-nominated *The First Time* (2012).

other *Star Wars* movie to date. We thought that one of the great things about Han was that he hearkened back to a Bogart-esque character who was always a little more complicated than the straight-up serial matinee idol George had originally found in Luke. We were leaning into the Han part of the universe, which was one where *everyone* had complicated motives. That actually led to a kind of female character who Larry was interested in, one essentially born out of 1940s crime movies. He described her as a character whose mind encompasses all of the other characters in the movie. She is wiser and savvier than they are capable of being. To have someone who was playing the various aspects of the situation against each other, who was in control more than Han even realized, was very exciting. It was different than Rey, and it was different than Leia—who was an idealist—and you wanted that from the get-go.

The other thing we felt pretty strongly about was that every one of the central relationships in the movie—which we really saw as Beckett, Qi'ra and Chewie—would have those positive or negative influences. I don't mean that literally, but like a positive charge or a negative based on his personality. Qi'ra abandoning Han would become a really seminal moment in his life, where he would learn that there were things more complicated

08

than his youthful, romantic impulses. We liked the idea that at the end of the movie, he had to outgrow both his idealistic, romantic ideas, and his ideas of loyalty related to Beckett. It was the moment when all those things slipped away and this Wookiee was standing next to him, totally loyal; his true friend. Crafting the movie so that it would all come together in that moment of him seeing betrayal, and heartbreak, and loyalty—fused into one crystallizing moment in his life—was a strong way, emotionally, for the movie to end.

You secured a surprise with Qi'ra's involvement with Crimson Dawn. Had you planned more surprises?
Oh yeah. We envisaged it as the beginning of her story, and not the end of their relationship, either. We could tell more stories about the two of them and how that relationship would ▶

05 Han's romance with Qi'ra will shape his future relationships. (Opposite page)

06 Chewbacca and Han with Lando's impounded starship.

07 On Savareen, Han will face life-altering choices.

08 Jonathan Kasdan on the *Solo* set..

09

09 Han and Chewie bond after their escape from Mimban.

"LARRY'S VOICE IS IN HAN THROUGH EACH OF THE MOVIES HE IS IN... THERE ARE THEMES AND IMPULSES THAT LARRY BRINGS TO THAT CHARACTER THAT ARE EVIDENT IN THE VERY EARLIEST STAGES OF HAN'S LIFE—AND THE VERY LAST."

▶ continue to evolve. We thought that they both represented different sides of the same coin. Qi'ra is able to make some of the tougher decisions that Han is not capable of making in favor of her ambitions, or her career, one might say. And Han is always stymied by his impulse to help people and to do the right thing. We felt like that story was just beginning to be told, and I think there's an appetite among the fans. There's a long future ahead of them, and I think there will be a lot of opportunities to tell a lot of stories. So, I'm excited about that.

To touch on a philosophical point, Han essentially helps inspire the Rebellion with his choices, but he also makes a conscious choice not to be part of it. Do you think that is something he's still running from in the original trilogy?
I think that he is. What, hopefully, is established at the end of the movie is that this is the primary conflict in his life—between that impulse and the more self-serving impulse which keeps coming back in the form of the Empire. I think there's something funny, and true, and real about a cause that someone just keeps continually—by fate or chance—bumping into, and keeps rejecting. I think that our hope in designing it, certainly if you were to watch the Han movie in sequence with the other films, would be to see a real arc to his feelings; from a young man rejecting the cause to embracing the cause; from rejecting his son to embracing his son; and finally dying, literally embracing his son. One of the things I think time will tell about *Solo* is that there is something really nice about the fact that, with the exception of *A New Hope*, Larry's voice is in Han through each of the movies he is in. There is a consistency there and it's really palpable. There are themes and impulses that Larry brings to that character that are evident in the very earliest stages of Han's life—and the very last.

It must be something to have watched your father's career, and now be part of it?
It's an amazing thing. *Star Wars*, in general, is such a humbling thing to be a part of. You can hear about it, and be near it, but once you're actually on the set, it's overwhelming. It isn't like anything else because the iconography of it is so powerful. To see Chewbacca sitting in the director's chair always makes it so you can't believe your life. It doesn't get much better than that. ☺

Fighting Talk!

THE STUNTS AND FIGHTING STYLES OF *SOLO: A STAR WARS STORY*

S olo: *A Star Wars Story* was a unique and challenging opportunity for the movie's stunt crew, which included action designer and 2nd unit director Brad Allen, stunt coordinator Mark Ginther, and fight coordinator Guillermo Grispo. Aside from thrilling action sequences that at times featured huge crowds and creature costumes—and all with practical effects— the team was also tasked with developing different fighting styles specific to each of the principal characters.

Guillermo Grispo and special effects supervisor Dominic Tuohy talk us through some of their challenges.

01 HAN SOLO

◆ "Everything we do must serve the story; the action must be character-driven," explains Guillermo Grispo, the fight coordinator on *Solo: A Star Wars Story* (2018). When it came to defining Han Solo's fighting style, Grispo and the stunt team wove in elements of military training to reflect Han's brief stint in the Imperial Army, combined with the rougher edges he picked up during a tough childhood on Corellia.

"Han Solo is a street fighter, with a mean swing," says Grispo. "He is opportunistic in everything he does to counter and to get out of trouble. He improvises, makes or creates weapons from any handy object, and he's agile. We also see him pick up some tricks from Beckett."

Han Solo's fighting style was a combination of street fighting and military training.

BECKETT

◆ "For Tobias Beckett, we borrowed the fight mannerisms of cowboys from the best Western films," says Grispo. "Woody Harrelson (Beckett) was very excited about the gunplay for this film. He put in a lot of hours learning how to twirl the guns, which is not that easy to do. The two six-shooters are pretty unique, and Woody was able to learn how to twirl and manipulate the guns to maximum effect in a display of very expressive gunplay."

02

CHEWBACCA

◆ For Chewbacca's style, Grispo reveals that, "Early on, we started to think about seeing a full-on display of Chewbacca's power. Is he as strong as an ox, or as strong as a bear? Once we had worked out those parameters, we were able to develop the cinematic action."

The stunt team took full advantage of Joonas Suotamo's athleticism when designing action sequences involving the mighty Wookiee. "Joonas was very quick to pick up the moves," notes Grispo, "and he loved to do it. That was a tremendous benefit to the stunt team."

Despite working to offer up something fresh and new with Chewbacca for audiences to enjoy, the Solo team felt a responsibility to ensure they maintained continuity of body language with Peter Mayhew's original portrayal of the character. To do this, they closely rewatched Mayhew's performances in the original *Star Wars* trilogy, the end result being a seamless transition between the two actors.

03

> "THE STUNT TEAM TOOK FULL ADVANTAGE OF JOONAS SUOTAMO'S ATHLETICISM WHEN DESIGNING ACTION SEQUENCES INVOLVING THE MIGHTY WOOKIEE."

04 MASTERS OF TERÄS KÄSI

◆ In *Solo: A Star Wars Story*, we learn that Qi'ra has been trained in Teräs Käsi by her boss, Dryden Vos—a practitioner of an extreme martial art that had previously only appeared in a *Star Wars* videogame. A key facet of the Teräs Käsi style is that it lends a fighter extreme speed and an aptitude for anticipating strikes from an opponent.

However, beyond animated pixels, the fighting style had never been truly defined. The *Solo* stunt team therefore needed to research and create Teräs Käsi from scratch, building its signature moves and use of weapons before they could teach Emilia Clarke (Qi'ra) and Paul Bettany (Dryden Vos).

The art department had designed exotic double-bladed daggers for Vos, the likes of which the stunt team had never seen before, so they tagged them as a Teräs Käsi trademark weapon, as well as Qi'ra's sword. Grispo says: "It has a pretty unique look. It almost looks like a fork combined with a sword, in that it has a separation within the blade."

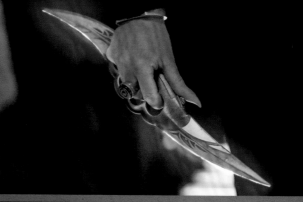

05

THE TRAIN HEIST

◆ Defining the physical attributes and fighting styles of the lead characters was only part of the stunt crew's job—they then had to be incorporated into thrilling, edge-of-the-seat action sequences. All stunt choreography has to be cinematically friendly, while adapting to the style, ability, and strengths of the cast, and the team had their work cut out for them staging the epic train heist on Vandor.

The train itself was nearly 40 feet long, 12 feet wide, and mounted on a huge gimble some 30 feet above the studio floor. The gimble itself was capable of moving from a zero position to plus and minus 15 degrees, then to 90 degrees on a cue, repeatedly—usually with the cast on board! It was a long and challenging sequence to shoot.

"Most gimbals give only 20 degrees of movement, so we had to build something bespoke," says special effects supervisor Dominic Tuohy. "We built a rig that weighed four tons and could move in two seconds. That's a lot of inertia, a lot of mechanical advantage and disadvantage to be in control of, while keeping the artists safe. It was quite a challenge." ✪

The conveyex set was 40 feet long and mounted on a gimble 30 feet above the studio floor.

"THE TEAM HAD THEIR WORK CUT OUT FOR THEM STAGING THE EPIC TRAIN HEIST ON VANDOR."

WANTED

HAN SOLO

HERO OR VILLAIN? THIS SPACE PIRATE HAS BEEN KNOWN TO SHOOT FIRST AND ASK QUESTIONS LATER. ONLY IN IT FOR THE MONEY?

APPEAL

A CERTAIN POINT OF VIEW

STAR WARS INSIDER CASTS AN EYE ON THE ROGUES AND SCOUNDRELS WHO LIVE ON THE MURKY EDGE BETWEEN GOOD AND EVIL.
WORDS: DANIEL WALLACE

WANTED

BOBA FETT

...LIED TO THE EMPIRE OR JUST THE HIGHEST
...DER FOR HIS SERVICES?

Jabba the Hutt and Bib Fortuna. Simply trying to make their way in the universe?

Dark side, light side—why do we have to choose? The real secret of *Star Wars'* popularity lies with the morally flexible characters on the fringe. These cunning rogues get to have their devil's food cake, and eat it, too!

"Your friend is quite a mercenary," sniffed Princess Leia in the movie that enshrined Han Solo in pop culture's pantheon of lovable scoundrels. "I wonder if he really cares about anything, or anyone." And while Han eventually revealed his underdog spirit, Leia's assessment reads like a spotter's guide to identifying the characters in the saga who spend their time as fringe dwellers.

In *Star Wars*, most heroes wear their hearts on their sleeves and the villains are sneering torturers with violent names like Maul and Savage. In Leia's eyes, the galactic conflict is clear-cut, its combatants arrayed into armies sporting white hats and black hats. Who better to complicate this worldview than an outsider who conceals his nobility beneath a thick layer of cynicism? Or, if you prefer the clothing metaphor, someone who wears a black vest over a white shirt?

Han Solo is far from the

Vilmarh Grahrk

only resident on the fringe. The opposing poles of good and evil are linked by a vast ocean of gray, expressed in shades that range from Han's wisecracking heroism to Cad Bane's cool competence.

What do all these fringers have in common? They're on the playing field but not wearing uniforms. If you watch long enough you'll see a fringer help one side or the other, but only when it helps the bottom line. It's a rare fringer indeed—with Han and Lando the exceptions that prove the rule—who decides to pack it in and join one of the two teams.

Dungeons & Dragons fans understand the urge to classify characters on a spectrum with "good and evil" on one axis and "lawful and chaotic" on the other. The *Star Wars* fringe appeals to anyone who ever rolled a character with neutral stats—the kind of bard who'd agree to fight the owlbear but only if it came with a guaranteed payout of gold pieces.

Most fringers care only about the credits, and it's their deal-making pragmatism that we recognize as the *lingua franca* of modern life. *Not everybody can save the world*, the fringer thinks. *Why not make some money in the meantime?*

Smugglers, crime-lords, bounty hunters,

Dengar, Han Solo , Watto, the Jawas, and Boba Fett ain't in it for the revolution—just their own survival in a tough galaxy!

on Tatooine, sufficiently distant from Coruscant's political turmoil that he doesn't even accept Republic currency.

Lando Calrissian is one fringer who tried to take Principle #1 to heart, keeping his head down on Cloud City until Darth Vader announced he was "altering the deal" to bring the outpost's residents under Imperial rule. Some *Star Wars* fans still blame Lando for selling out Han Solo, but as Cloud City's baron administrator, Lando had the unenviable task of protecting five million people. Think of all the Ugnaughts and tibanna gas miners—not to mention Willrow Hood, Cloud City's famous Ice Cream Guy—the next time you condemn Lando for trying to maintain Bespin's low profile in the shadows of the fringe.

and proprietors of "honest businesses" all agree on one thing—you've got to stay flexible if you want to stay afloat. The principles of life on the fringe make a pretty good code of conduct, if you don't mind being labeled as slightly shady!

PRINCIPLE #1: KEEP YOUR HEAD DOWN!

The stakes in *Star Wars* are so epic that a simple door-to-door search for a missing droid might result in your house getting burnt down. In a galaxy where the good guys and bad guys fight battles that can depopulate planets, why make yourself a target? The inhabitants of the fringe know that there's money to be made amid the mayhem, just as long as they resist the temptation to run off and enlist. Watto is one of these pragmatists. The pot-bellied Toydarian makes a comfortable living operating a junk shop in Mos Espa

PRINCIPLE #2: YOU CAN'T HAVE IT ALL.

Fringers are realists. They weren't adopted into royalty. They didn't receive magic swords from wise old mentors. And they certainly weren't conceived by the midi-chlorians to bring balance to the Force. They're normal people, born without superpowers or silver spoons, who survive by being shrewd.

I'd argue that fringers are the smartest people in the *Star Wars* saga, if you define intelligence as street smarts. Padmé Amidala or Senator Bail Organa would be fine choices if you wanted to hold a state dinner for the Pantoran ambassador, but to dig up real dirt on the Pantorans, give me a smuggler or a street rat any day. Because most fringers don't know where their next paycheck is coming from, they have to be flexible, inventive, and hungry. There's no

Rodians and Jawas might not seem to have much in common, but in the *Star Wars* galaxy alliances are often formed in mutual self interest. Below, HK-47 is proof that fringers are not always organic!

tenure on the fringe, and nothing to fall back on if you lose an assignment to a sharper competitor.

Smugglers are the poster children of this mindset. Han and Chewie accept a lot of jobs from Jabba, but at the end of the day they're freelancers. Their "have ship, will travel" lifestyle is the subject of the classic Han Solo novels by Brian Daley, in which Han and Chewie struggle to patch up the *Millennium Falcon* while negotiating fees from clients with names like Big Bunji and Ploovo Two-For-One.

PRINCIPLE #3:
MONEY MAKES THE WORLD GO AROUND.
In *Star Wars* speak the above song from *Cabaret* might be re-titled "Credits Keep

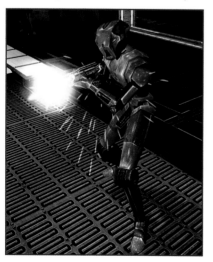

the Galactic Disc Spinning." But the truth remains—while the other factions are motivated by ideology, the thing that unites all fringers is the allure of cold, hard cash.

Leia knew this— remember her "mercenary" comment— and so did Luke, who enticed Han into an armed rescue by promising "more wealth than you can imagine." Selfish? Sure, but it's also a very human motivation, and one that we all understand to some degree. It's why Han's greed gets a big audience laugh, and why we smile when Watto puts the kibosh on a Jedi Master's mind-whammy with the ultimatum, "No money, no parts, no deal."

PRINCIPLE #4:
SOMEBODY'S GOT TO DO IT!
Without the fringers populating the emptiness between good and evil's moral extremes, nothing of consequence would ever get done. Smugglers stay in business because there's a demand, since the Trade Federation's tariffs are choking off supply. Demand probably doubles during wartime and the shipping disruptions it brings, and in the *Star Wars* galaxy "wartime" fills 11 months out of every 12.

With every regime passing new laws, it's not surprising to see so much outsourcing.

Chewbacca, Cad Bane, Embo, and Sugi. Quite the mercenaries in their own separate ways.

Want to go somewhere? Book passage with a smuggler. In need of a cop? Try a bounty hunter. Looking for something dangerous and in violation of Imperial law? Peruse the wares in a Hutt's back alley bazaar. On Tatooine you can take care of all three of these with a single visit to Mos Eisley's seedier section.

In fact, if the fringe were to have a capital it would surely be Tatooine. Here, Hutt crime-lords like Jabba and Gardulla control the upper rungs of the black-market economy, while roving Jawa tribes scavenge everything that falls to the bottom. Their willingness to do whatever it takes to survive means that the fringers may be the only ones still standing at the end of the latest war.

Bounty hunters deserve a special mention for their role on the fringe. While they're usually grouped with the villains, their "just business" attitude disqualifies them from comparison with true believers like General Grievous or Darth Sidious. If Boba Fett accepts more jobs from the Empire than from the Rebels, it's only because the Empire pays better.

This fact underlies what might be the biggest strategic error of the Clone Wars. If the Republic and the Jedi didn't spend all their time fighting Cad Bane, Asajj Ventress, Embo, and their bounty-hunting comrades, they might realize that they could easily turn their enemies into allies by dipping into the Republic's treasury.

It brings to mind Dark Helmet's line from Mel Brooks' *Spaceballs*: "Now you will see that evil will always triumph, because good is dumb." Fringers see the truth in this, but also recognize that the villains are just as thick-headed. Bound by their own rules, the good guys and bad guys are just as concerned with *how* a victory occurs as they are with whether a victory occurs at all. By contrast, for fringers the ends always justify the means.

PRINCIPLE #5: FRINGERS MAKE EVERYTHING BETTER.

Because the *Star Wars* saga is an epic struggle between good and evil, the action focuses on these combatants almost exclusively. That's why Han "I ain't in this for your revolution" Solo was such a hit in the original trilogy.

Beyond the movies and *The Clone Wars* series, many memorable fringers have starred in the *Star Wars* Expanded Universe. Fast-talking con artists like Marn Hierogryph and Vilmarh Grahrk have livened up the comics, while games have given us such gray-morality characters as the wickedly funny assassin droid HK-47. In the upcoming massively multiplayer online game *Star Wars*: The Old Republic, players have to pledge their allegiance to either the Republic or the Sith, but can then customize their character with a fringer class like smuggler or bounty hunter.

Hopefully these are signs of a brighter spotlight on fringe characters in the future, for fringers are the only people who can pop up in any era of *Star Wars* history. Every time a Sith Lord blows up a planet, a hundred fringers will be there, trying to make a fast buck by selling the planetary fragments as souvenir paperweights.⚙

STAR WARS LIBRARY

- *ROGUE ONE: A STAR WARS STORY* THE OFFICIAL COLLECTOR'S EDITION
- *ROGUE ONE: A STAR WARS STORY* THE OFFICIAL MISSION DEBRIEF
- *STAR WARS: THE LAST JEDI* THE OFFICIAL COLLECTOR'S EDITION
- *STAR WARS: THE LAST JEDI* THE OFFICIAL MOVIE COMPANION
- *STAR WARS: THE LAST JEDI* THE ULTIMATE GUIDE
- *SOLO: A STAR WARS STORY* THE OFFICIAL COLLECTOR'S EDITION

- *SOLO: A STAR WARS STORY* THE ULTIMATE GUIDE
- THE BEST OF *STAR WARS INSIDER* VOLUME 1
- THE BEST OF *STAR WARS INSIDER* VOLUME 2
- THE BEST OF *STAR WARS INSIDER* VOLUME 3
- THE BEST OF *STAR WARS INSIDER* VOLUME 4
- *STAR WARS:* LORDS OF THE SITH
- *STAR WARS:* HEROES OF THE FORCE

- *STAR WARS:* ICONS OF THE GALAXY
- *STAR WARS:* THE SAGA BEGINS
- *STAR WARS* THE ORIGINAL TRILOGY
- *STAR WARS:* ROGUES, SCOUNDRELS AND BOUNTY HUNTERS (SEPT '19)
- *STAR WARS* CREATURES, ALIENS, AND DROIDS (NOV '19)
- *STAR WARS: THE RISE OF SKYWALKER* THE OFFICIAL COLLECTOR'S EDITION (DEC '19)

STAR WARS
THE SAGA BEGINS

STAR WARS:
THE RISE OF SKYWALKER
(DEC '19)

MARVEL LIBRARY

X-MEN
THE DARK PHOENIX SAGA (MAY '20)

NOVELS
- ANT-MAN NATURAL ENEMY
- AVENGERS EVERYBODY WANTS TO RULE THE WORLD
- AVENGERS INFINITY (NOV '19)
- BLACK PANTHER WHO IS THE BLACK PANTHER?
- CAPTAIN AMERICA DARK DESIGNS (OCT '19)
- CAPTAIN MARVEL LIBERATION RUN (OCT '19)
- CIVIL WAR
- DEADPOOL PAWS
- SPIDER-MAN FOREVER YOUNG
- SPIDER-MAN HOSTILE TAKEOVER
- SPIDER-MAN KRAVEN'S LAST HUNT
- THANOS DEATH SENTENCE
- VENOM LETHAL PROTECTOR
- X-MEN DAYS OF FUTURE PAST

MARVEL STUDIOS:
THE FIRST TEN YEARS

MOVIE SPECIALS
- MARVEL STUDIOS' ANT MAN & THE WASP
- MARVEL STUDIOS' AVENGERS: ENDGAME
- MARVEL STUDIOS' AVENGERS: INFINITY WAR
- MARVEL STUDIOS' BLACK PANTHER (COMPANION)
- MARVEL STUDIOS' BLACK PANTHER (SPECIAL)
- MARVEL STUDIOS' CAPTAIN MARVEL
- MARVEL STUDIOS' SPIDER-MAN: FAR FROM HOME
- MARVEL STUDIOS: THE FIRST TEN YEARS
- MARVEL STUDIOS' THOR: RAGNAROK

SPIDER-MAN: INTO THE SPIDERVERSE

ARTBOOKS
- MARVEL'S *SPIDER-MAN* THE ART OF THE GAME
- MARVEL: *CONQUEST OF CHAMPIONS* THE ART OF THE BATTLEREALM
- *SPIDER-MAN: INTO THE SPIDERVERSE*
- THE ART OF IRON MAN 10TH ANNIVERSARY EDITION

DISNEY LIBRARY

DISNEY *DUMBO*
THE OFFICIAL MOVIE SPECIAL

DISNEY•PIXAR *TOY STORY 4*
THE OFFICIAL MOVIE SPECIAL

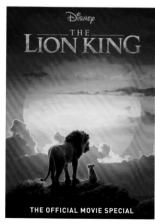

DISNEY *THE LION KING*
THE OFFICIAL MOVIE SPECIAL
(JULY '19)

DISNEY *FROZEN 2*
THE OFFICIAL MOVIE SPECIAL
(OCT '19)

AVAILABLE AT ALL GOOD BOOKSTORES AND ONLINE

TITAN-COMICS.COM | TITANBOOKS.COM